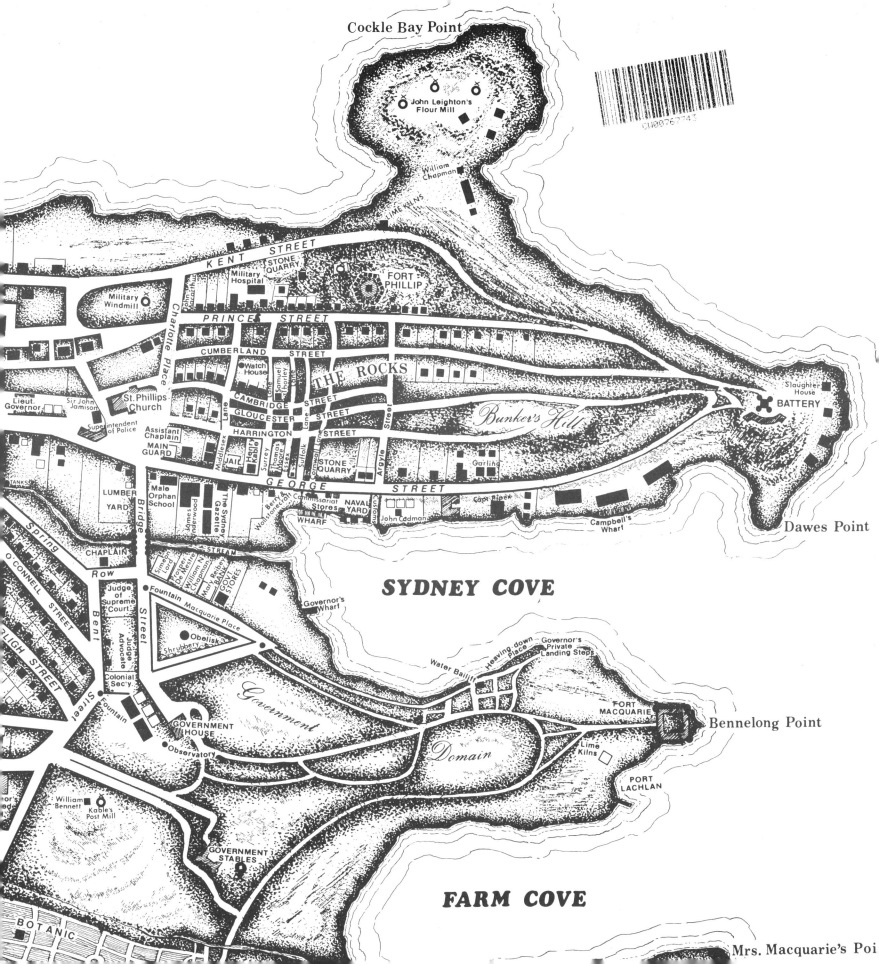

Cockle Bay Point

John Leighton's
Flour Mill

William
Chapman

LIME KILNS

KENT STREET

Military
Windmill

Military
Hospital

STONE
QUARRY

FORT
PHILLIP

PRINCES STREET

CUMBERLAND STREET

Charlotte Place

Watch
House

Samuel
Thorley

THE ROCKS

Lieut.
Governor

Sir John
Jamison

St. Phillips
Church

Superintendent
of Police

CAMBRIDGE STREET

GLOUCESTER STREET

HARRINGTON STREET

Bunker's Hill

Slaughter
House

BATTERY

Assistant
Chaplain

MAIN
GUARD

JAIL

Henry
Kable

Middlesex Lane

Surrey

Thomas
Essex

Suffolk

Cumberland Lane

Argyle Street

STONE
QUARRY

Garling

TANKS

LUMBER
YARD

Bridge Street

Male
Orphan
School

James
Underwood

The Sydney
Gazette

Berry &
Wollstonecraft

GEORGE STREET

Commissariat
Stores

NAVAL
YARD

Custom

John Cadman

Capt. Piper

Campbell's
Wharf

Dawes Point

Spring Row

CHAPLAIN

STREAM

Simeon
Lord

Prosper
De Mestre

William N.
Chapman

Mary Reibey

BANK

GOVT
STORES

SYDNEY COVE

O'CONNELL STREET

Bent Street

Judge
of
Supreme
Court

Fountain

Macquarie Place

Governor's
Wharf

BLIGH STREET

Judge
Advocate

Colonial
Sec'y

Obelisk

Shrubbery

Water Bailiff

Heaving down
Place

Governor's
Private
Landing Steps

FORT
MACQUARIE

Bennelong Point

Fountain

GOVERNMENT
HOUSE

Observatory

Government

Domain

Lime
Kilns

PORT
LACHLAN

William
Bennett

Kable's
Post Mill

GOVERNMENT
STABLES

FARM COVE

BOTANIC

Mrs. Macquarie's Poi

HISTORIC SYDNEY

THE FOUNDING OF AUSTRALIA

PUBLISHED BY PANDANUS PRESS
Cutty Sark Studio
10 Matingara Street
Chapel Hill, Brisbane Q. 4069.
PHONE: 07-3378-2744. FAX: 07-3378-2744

DISTRIBUTED BY TOWER BOOKS (French's Forest, Sydney)
PHONE: 02 9975-5566. FAX: 02-9975 5599.

Text copyright © Susanna de Vries, 1983.
Design © Susanna de Vries and Neysa Moss.
Jacket design © Jake de Vries.

First published by Doubleday Australia Pty Ltd in 1983 under the title 'HISTORIC SYDNEY AND ITS EARLY ARTISTS'.
2nd edition published under the above title by Angus & Robertson, Sydney in 1987
3rd and revised edition of 2000 copies only, published by Pandanus Press, Brisbane, 1999 as HISTORIC SYDNEY — THE FOUNDING OF AUSTRALIA.

National Library of Australia
Cataloguing-in-publication
De Vries, Susanna
  Historic Sydney: The founding of Australia
  Revised edition
  Bibliography
  Includes index
  ISBN. 0 9585408 2 9

  1. Sydney (N.S.W.) in art. 2. Early artists of Australia.
  3. Historic buildings - New South Wales - Sydney.
  4. Painting, Australian colonial. I. Title. Historic Sydney:
  II. Title. The founding of Australia.
758'.1

Typeset in Plantin.
Printed in Singapore by Kyodo Printing Company.

Historic Sydney
The Founding of Australia

Susanna de Vries

PANDANUS PRESS

Contents

Introduction:

Working as Head of the Department of Rare Books in a leading Sydney art auction house and having access to private and public art collections I was able to put together this selection of historically important paintings and engravings of Sydney. In the 1980s under the title *Historic Sydney and its Early Artists*, the book went into two editions, both of which sold out. By popular demand Pandanus Press was requested to publish an updated edition with a different subtitle.

Since the book was first published, prices of colonial art soared and many that were privately owned changed hands, including those Conrad Martens paintings formerly owned by Australian Consolidated Press Holdings, sold to Mr Alan Bond and then resold. Increased interest in Sydney history has seen a Museum of Sydney on the site of Old Government House and the Hyde Park Barracks turned into a fascinating museum of convict life.

Since I started writing this book Sydney has become a centre for international tourism and there has been a far greater awareness of its unique charm and history. The Queen Victoria Building, on the site of the old George Street markets, has been renovated, so I have updated its history, and also added a view of the Royal Botanical Gardens, which have recently celebrated their 170th birthday.

More views of the first buildings and streets of Sydney were painted than of any other capital city in the world. Due to the foresight of several great collectors, the majority of the paintings and their related engravings have been preserved in private collections and libraries. This is the first time that so many have been assembled in book form to show the development of the primitive convict settlement into a magnificent harbour city.

In April 1766 William Reeves marketed the first portable box of watercolour blocks and, by the time the First Fleet sailed, painting in watercolour had become a popular pastime. Artists no longer needed to prepare their own pigments to sketch outdoors, nor did they have to trail canvas and easels around with them on foot or on horseback and many amateurs took up the new "watercolour drawing."

Captain Hunter and Lieutenant Bradley painted Sydney Cove in its very first months of settlement while the skilled forger, Thomas Watling, recorded the bush tracks and slab huts of Sydney's first decade. In contrast, no museum or gallery holds a view of London's first streets by a Roman centurion, a Saxon settler or a Norman knight. The first known drawing of London was made to illustrate Chaucer's *Canterbury Tales* by a printer named Wynkin de Worde in 1497, when the thousand-year-old city stretched from Westminster to Greenwich. A puritanical fear of the arts probably inhibited the Pilgrim Fathers from commissioning any early views of American cities. New York was only drawn for the first time by Jasper Danckaerts when it had been settled for 50 years.

From first settlement, Sydney's governors had a totally different policy. Convicted forgers like Watling, Richard Read and Joseph Lycett were actively encouraged to paint views of the new town and some were sent to important officials in London, probably as a subtle form of propaganda for the success of Sydney's building programme.

Naval and military officers like Lieutenant Bradley, Captains Hunter and Wallis and Major Taylor produced accurate and detailed paintings of the first years of Australia. At their academies they had followed courses in topographical drawing, where they were taught by professional artists of repute "to render the significant features of a landscape interesting and of value in planning a naval or military operation." Their drawings and those of their talented French and Spanish counterparts like Lesueur, de Sainson, Arago and Brambilla, who visited Sydney on scientific expeditions, were used on return to their own countries, in the same way that aerial reconnaissance photographs record information obtained from space flights today.

With the increase in immigration the demand for Sydney views grew proportionately. John Carmichael, convict artist and engraver wrote that his market was the "numerous and respectable body of emigrants, with a circle of friends at home, eager to see everything respecting the distant abode of their relations." Artists like Prout, Terry, Gill and Fowles catered for Sydney inhabitants who wanted an inexpensive lithograph or engraving to send home, showing everyday life in Sydney, with its taverns, shops, cottages and streets. Fowles said that he drew "to remove the erroneous and discreditable notions current in England concerning the city of Sydney and to endeavour to represent Sydney as it really is." Conrad Martens specialised in painting harbour views and stately homes for the wealthy to purchase, while the observant and humorous Augustus Earle mingled with both rich and poor. Commissioned to paint the portraits of the rich, he drew the aboriginal 'King of Sydney' and the convicts in chains for his own interest, and Samuel Elyard painted the windmills of early Sydney for his own pleasure.

These prints and paintings provide detailed information about Sydney's first homes, paddle-wheel ferries, hansom cabs, windmills and horse-buses. They also show the muddy estuary of the Tank Stream and the dramatic change in the shape of the city as its mudflats were filled in to form Circular Quay. Selection of these historic paintings has necessarily been time-consuming, since for the purpose of this book a naive and relatively unknown sketch may be just as important as a well-known Martens. Some suburbs seem to have no known early paintings, while other areas attracted a great many. I have tried to include works by interesting but relatively unknown artists like Lord Henry Scott, Spong, Brambilla and Elliot Johnson. The innovations of the Sirius Cove group of the Australian "Impressionist" school resulted in a move away from eighteenth and nineteenth century topographical conventions. As their main works fall just outside Sydney's first hundred years, they are not included.

The convict and colonial topographical artists in this book present a unique, detailed and accurate record of social life in Sydney before the widespread use of the camera largely replaced their skills.

The Founding of Australia

This combined plan and drawing by convict Francis Fowkes, made three months after the arrival of the First Fleet, acts as a visual key to Lieutenant William Bradley's drawing. Fowkes, a young man of some education, had been given a seven-year sentence for stealing a coat and a pair of boots. His elegant plan shows the eastern side of Sydney Cove, reserved by Governor Phillip for his own portable but leaky prefabricated residence, which Fowkes described somewhat sarcastically as "The Governor's Mansion." Around him, Phillip laid out the future administrative section of Sydney when he designated this area for officers and their male and female convict servants. The Stream, later known as the Tank Stream, after holding tanks had been cut in it, was one of Governor Phillip's main reasons for leaving Botany Bay for Sydney Cove. It also formed a convenient social gulf between the officers and the mass of the great unwashed, who were left to fend for themselves at The Rocks. The stigma this gave to The Rocks area lasted for a century.

The male and female convict camps were close together near the intersection of today's George and Essex Streets. "What a scene of whoredom is going on there in the women's camp" wrote one marine officer. "No sooner has one man gone in with a woman but another goes with her." The marine encampment for 250 men was also situated nearby, at what is today the junction of George and Grosvenor Streets, and their slab huts and tents were hidden among the trees. The convicts were each given a length of canvas and told to fend for themselves. Some, rather than camp, made primitive huts of wattle and mud described by a female convict "as the most miserable huts you can possibly conceive." "The Governor's Mansion" was the only building with panes of glass in its windows. Everyone else made do with a lattice of twigs for privacy and inadequate protection from the flies and mosquitoes of Sydney's high summer.

Collins described the roofs as thatched with rushes and covered with clay, but "the weight of the clay and heavy rain soon destroyed them." And in summer 1788, it rained a great deal. "Save for the natural setting around the finest harbour in the world, everything was wretched, the tents ... sagging in a downpour, the night fires in the region of The Rocks, a sink of evil already and more like a gypsy encampment, the stumps and fallen trees and boggy tracks wending their way around rock and precipice," wrote Elizabeth Macarthur two years later, proving that things did not change too quickly around Sydney Cove.

It was hardly surprising, considering that there were over 1,000 people to house and only three trained carpenters among them. It also explains why Bradley drew his convict huts and the temporary prefabricated hospital, on what is now George Street, as if they were about to fall over in the next storm. After many thatched roofs fell in, Governor Phillip ordered that all huts were to be roofed with wooden shingles. Fowkes marked the convict "Shingling Parties" near the Brickfields, situated near today's Parramatta Road, and a stone quarry cut out of land which became the Domain. To the south is the farm which gave its name to Farm Cove. Vines, oranges, apples and pears brought from Rio and the Cape were all planted, but the soil was so poor that the place was eventually abandoned in favour of the more fertile soil of Parramatta.

The two artists may even have met at Sydney Cove, although Lieutenant Bradley arrived on board the *Sirius,* with the status of a naval officer and Fowkes came in chains on the *Alexander.* Francis Fowkes, as the prodigal son of a respected London merchant, was given a clerical position in the Governor's secretariat rather than a labouring job and, in 1794, was granted a large block of land near Windsor. His historic map returned to England with the First Fleet, as did the young Lieutenant Bradley, who left a permanent mark on Sydney by naming Bradley's Head after himself, on his expedition to chart the virgin bush of Mosman. The historic Australian and South Pacific maps that he made with Captain John Hunter have become collector's items worth thousands of dollars today, and he finished his career as a Rear-Admiral.

However, he seems to have suffered from some pre-senile dementia and committed a series of petty frauds on Her Majesty Queen Victoria's mail service which were ludicrously easy to detect. Today he would have been given psychiatric treatment and the whole affair hushed up, but in 1814, during the Napoleonic Wars, he was sentenced to death. His wife petitioned for a remission and he escaped transportation in chains back to Sydney Cove. He received a pardon on condition he went into exile for life. His requests to return to England fell on deaf ears and he spent a bitter nineteen years in exile in France before he died, a lonely and forgotten man.

Today Fowkes' map and Bradley's drawing of Sydney Cove in 1788 are part of the treasures of the Mitchell Library and are two of the most valuable items of Australiana preserved there, since they constitute the first eye-witness accounts of the birth of a nation.

Plate 1
LIEUTENANT WILLIAM BRADLEY.
Sydney Cove 1788. *Original drawing
Mitchell Library.*

Plate 2
FRANCIS FOWKES. **Sydney Cove,
1788.** *Mitchell Library.*

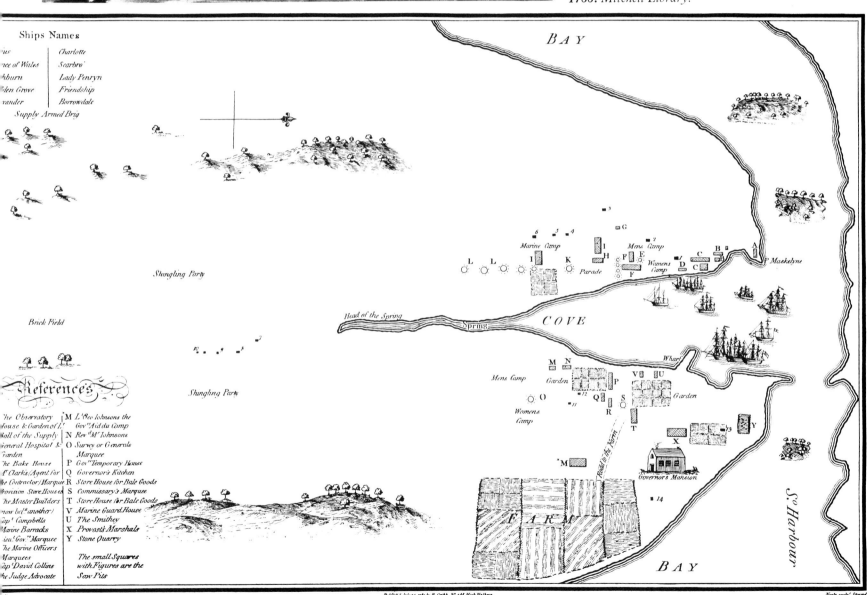

Ships Names

ius	*Charlotte*
ce of Wales	*Scarbro'*
hburn	*Lady Penryn*
den Grove	*Friendship*
rander	*Borrowdale*
Supply Armed Brig	

BAY

Shingling Party

Brick Field

Head of the Spring

Spring

COVE

Marine Camp

Parade

Mens Camp

Womens Camp

P. Maskelyne

Shingling Party

Mens Camp

Garden

Womens Camp

Wharf

Garden

Road to the Farm

Governor's Mansion

FARM

S.t Harbour

BAY

References

The Observatory	M L.t Geo Johnsons the
House & Garden of L.t	Gov.rs Aid du Camp
Hall of the Supply	N Rev.d M.r Johnsons
General Hospital &	O Survey.or Generals
Garden	Marquee
The Bake House	P Gov.rs Temporary House
M.r Clarks (Agent for	Q Governor's Kitchen
the Contractor) Marquee	R Store House for Bale Goods
Provision Store Houses	S Commissary's Marquee
The Master Builders	T Store House for Bale Goods
now bel.d to another)	V Marine Guard House
Cap.t Campbells	U The Smithey
Marine Barracks	X Provosts Marshals
Lieu.t Gov.r Marquee	Y Stone Quarry
The Marine Officers	
Marquees	The small Squares
Cap.t David Collins	with Figures are the
the Judge Advocate	Saw Pits

Publish'd July 24 1789 by R Cribb N.o 288 High Holborn

Noble sculp.t Strand

Sketch & Description of the Settlement at **Sydney Cove Port Jackson** *in the* **County** *of* **Cumberland** *taken*

by a transported Convict on the 16.th of April, 1788 which was not quite 3 Months after Commodore Phillips's Landing there

George Street,
Australia's First High Street.

Plate 3

These two views are believed to be painted from sketches by Thomas Watling, Australia's first professional artist. With a fourteen-year sentence for forgery, he arrived in Sydney in 1792. His talents were recognised and he was immediately assigned as a servant to John White, the principal surgeon. White had just published his own account of the founding of Australia and forced Watling to make numerous illustrations for another book, which was never published. Some of these 'Watling Drawings' are now in the British Museum of National History in London.

Watling detested White and described himself as "a genius in bondage to a very mercenary, sordid person." He also complained bitterly that he was "lent about as an household utensil to his (employer's) neighbours." One of Watling's "borrowers" was Judge-Advocate David Collins, whose published "Account of the English Colony in New South Wales," was to include a series of unattributed illustrations of Sydney's first streets, from drawings made by Watling. Publishers and writers in the eighteenth century had no concept of copyright and were under no legal constraint whatsoever to acknowledge the work of an obscure convict. The engraved illustration above and the aquatint on the facing page, from the collection of the Mitchell Library, were both redrawn and "improved" for engraving by Edward Dayes, a talented artist whose desperate poverty forced him to accept this type of copying from London publishers. Before he committed

suicide, depressed by lack of appreciation of his own watercolours, Dayes wrote a bitter attack on the system of redrawing the work of other artists for publication, without either acknowledgement or payment to the original artist. This lack of attribution makes it impossible today to be absolutely certain that Dayes copied Watling, but there is a Watling drawing in the Mitchell Library, which appears definitely to be the missing link. Both the Watling and Dayes' views are made from Dawes Point looking along the part of George Street, named on Surveyor Meehan's 1807 map as "The High Street". In Watling's time this dirt track ran along the flat ledge below The Rocks ridge. It connected the Convict Hospital with the Military Barracks and the water supply of the Tank Stream. In 1804 Surgeon Thomson was on leave in London and provided this invaluable key with the lay-out of Sydney's first streets, homes and administrative buildings. Back Row became Phillip Street, Chapel Row became Castlereagh Street and Pitts' Row is now Pitt Street.

Watling planned to compile a book of his own paintings. This was never published, but the scenes he painted are today some of Australia's rarest and most valuable early historical records. In this important aquatint with its key, a ship is under construction at the government shipyard, near today's Cadman's Cottage where so many famous early Australian ships were built.

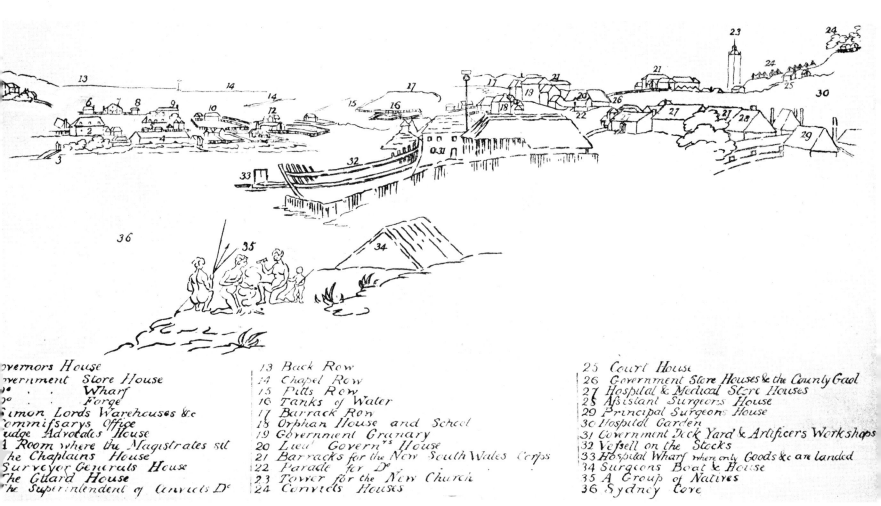

	13 Back Row	25 Court House
vernors House	14 Chapel Row	26 Government Store Houses & the County Gaol
vernment Store House	15 Pitts Row	27 Hospital & Medical Store Houses
o. Wharf	16 Tanks of Water	28 Assistant Surgeons House
o. Forge	17 Barrack Row	29 Principal Surgeons House
imon Lords Warehouses &c	18 Orphan House and School	30 Hospital Garden
ommissarys Office	19 Government Granary	31 Government Dock Yard & Artificers Workshops
udge Advocates House	20 Lieu Govern.rs House	32 Vessell on the Stocks
1 Room where the Magistrates sit	21 Barracks for the New South Wales Corps	33 Hospital Wharf where only Goods &c are landed
he Chaplains House	22 Parade for D.o	34 Surgeons Boat & House
Surveyor Generals House	23 Tower for the New Church	35 A Group of Natives
The Guard House	24 Convicts Houses	36 Sydney Cove
he Superintendent of Convicts D.o		

Plate 4

Plate 5

Captions for Plates 3, 4 & 5: see over

Australia's First Hospital

The surveyor and explorer of the Blue Mountains, George William Evans, made one of the most important paintings of early Sydney, showing the rear of the Convict Hospital on George Street North. Three days after the arrival of the First Fleet, Surgeon John White recorded that there were so many sick convicts that it was necessary to build a hospital for them. Governor Phillip ordered a vegetable garden to be planted beside this hospital to try to counteract the numerous cases of scurvy. In July 1788 Surgeon White was writing of his "dreadful sick-list" of nearly five hundred patients suffering from typhoid, dysentery, and infection of flesh wounds after severe floggings, as well as malnutrition and venereal disease.

Undoubtedly the most harrowing event ever witnessed at Australia's first hospital was the arrival of the hordes of sick and dying from the Second Fleet in 1790. An officer of the Second Fleet wrote in his diary that "the slave trade is merciful compared with what I have seen aboard this Fleet". He was right, since in the slave trade there was at least a good profit motive for the ships' captains to keep the slaves alive and in reasonable health for sale on arrival in America. In contrast, Australian convicts had no re-sale value and the only profit for the captains of the Second Fleet and other transport ships lay in selling off the unconsumed portions of the convicts' rations when they reached Sydney. In their turn the convicts augmented their meagre daily rations with those of the dead, concealing the death of another convict until the body was already rotting in its chains to spread yet more disease through the convict ships. These small hospital buildings were totally inadequate to receive the additional five hundred patients from the Second Fleet, who were brought ashore at the Hospital Wharf. The majority of them had to be carried ashore, since they were too weak to walk. Many convicts died of exposure when the holds were opened and they came up on deck for the first time. Their pitiful corpses lay on the foreshore of The Rocks for days, before they were finally rowed over to the North Shore for burial.

About ninety tents occupied the grassy area behind the George Street Hospital, each tent containing four people, the majority "covered in filth, lice and their own nastiness" as the chaplain to the fleet described them. There were no beds available, since the Hospital was full to overflowing, and in the depths of winter these sick men were laid on the grass beside the Hospital, with only one blanket to every four men. As each man died, so the others seized his clothing or his blanket, if he was one of the fortunate who had one. Gangrene set in to many of their wounds, and amputation without anaesthetics was the only remedy the surgeons could offer.

The temporary hospital seen here with its dividing sections clearly showing, was brought out on a ship called the *Justinian*, which fortunately arrived ahead of the rest of the second fleet. Governor Phillip wrote that it was erected with great difficulty by twelve convicts and sixteen ships' carpenters. However, its foundations were made of wood and rotted away fast in Sydney's humid summer conditions.

At the time when he made this painting, George William Evans was Acting Assistant Surveyor and lived in the Surveyor's cottage beside the Hospital, while Surveyor Meehan was absent on leave. Evans' experience in surveying ensures that his view is one of the most accurate of Old Sydney Town. Following the trail of Blaxland and Wentworth, he was the first to actually cross the Great Dividing Range, which opened up new grazing lands and substantially affected the future prosperity of Australia.

Plate 3
Attrib. THOMAS WATLING. **The first View of George Street.** *Copper engraving from David Collins "Account of the English Colony in New South Wales."*

Plates 4 & 5
Attrib. THOMAS WATLING. **Sydney in 1802.** *Lithograph with key. Redrawn by Edward Dayes. Mitchell Library.*

Plate 6 GEORGE WILLIAM EVANS, *(attributed)* **Sydney Cove in 1803.** *Unsigned watercolour. Dixson Galleries. □ Sir William Dixson once owned this remarkable painting originally presented to Viscount Sydney c. 1805. On the extreme left are the cottages of the Principal and Assistant Surgeons, while the cottage with the large chimney was once inhabited by Surgeon William Redfern.*

The Convict Hospital and Medical Stores used these three long low buildings and the one on the right was the temporary hospital brought out from London by the Second Fleet in 1790. The lines along its walls show where the sections were joined together in Sydney. By the time that Evans drew it, this hospital was disease-ridden, filthy and airless, lacking in sanitation and with its tiny windows totally unsuitable for the climate. Just below the temporary hospital was the house of Isaac Nicholls, which six years later became Australia's first post office.

The tents for the dying convicts of the Second Fleet were pitched on the grass in the foreground. Evans made his painting from a site near today's Globe and Harrington Streets and shows how the hospital's three buildings extended along George Street North, past today's Surgeon's Court down to Argyle Street. This painting presents the clearest surviving image of the triangle of mudflats created by the Tank Stream estuary, which were eventually filled in to create Circular Quay. It reveals how wide the estuary became at low tide when the mudflats stretched to the Government Wharf. It also shows the stone bridge over the Tank Stream. In 1803 Bridge Street was surrounded by the residences of the colonial officials and the first storehouses of the Colony. The low building lying close to the bridge was the main guardhouse.

11

A French Spy at Sydney Cove

This elegant engraving made in 1802 by Lieutenant Charles Alexandre Lesueur, was the result of a Napoleonic political intrigue. Lesueur had trained as a navigator at his Naval and Military Academy but he had also taken a course in drawing. He was 22 years old when the *Geographe* and the *Naturaliste* were commissioned by the Emperor Napoleon to undertake scientific exploration in the South Seas under the command of the aging Captain Nicholas Baudin. Also on board was the famous French zoologist, Francois Peron, an expert on ethnology, who wished to study Australian Aboriginals and their customs as well as the plant life of Australia. Peron was to infuse Lesueur with his own enthusiasm for these subjects and change the young lieutenant's life.

Napoleon, although interested in scientific exploration and the international prestige that it conferred on France, had a deeper political purpose. Already locked in conflict with Britain for power in Europe, he was looking for new sources of wealth through colonial expansion. All drawings, maps and charts made on this scientific expedition had to be lodged with the French Admiralty on the expedition's return "for official inspection" before they could be published in an illustrated history of the voyage. This history was eventually published in 1807, complete with a folio-sized atlas containing drawings by Lesueur, Nicholas Petit and Peron. Lesueur, who was originally engaged as a helmsman on the expedition, with his aptitude for drawing was appointed to help Peron draw the thousands of zoological and botanical samples that the expedition acquired. Since there were no cameras, Lesueur was ordered to make topographical drawings of certain places, including Sydney, which accompanied the highly detailed report that was sent to the French Admiralty and probably to Napoleon. The reason for Napoleon's interest in a possible invasion of Sydney was its strategic importance as a harbour. Pacific whaling and sealing had become the wealthy growth industries of the early nineteenth century causing Napoleon to cast envious eyes on the area for a possible French whaling and sealing colony.

As early as 1791, convict transports arriving in Sydney had sighted large numbers of whales. The master of the *Britannia* assured Governor Phillip that he had seen more whales in the area on one voyage than "during six years on the Brazilian and American coasts." Captain Ebor Bunker, an American whaler, was even more enthusiastic for the new whaling and sealing grounds and in 1801 took home over 155 tons of whale oil and a cargo of whalebone from one voyage, using Sydney as his home port.

Seal fur lined ladies' cloaks and men's overcoats in Britain, Europe and North America, while whale oil was used for lamps and whalebone for the corsets so essential for ladies of fashion. Sydney merchants grew rich from whaling, sealing and supplying food and provisions to foreign ships that used Sydney as a port. In 1813, years after Baudin's visit, a French spy defected to Britain, claiming that he had details of a Napoleonic plot to invade Sydney to provide a French supply base in the South Seas. The plot was found to be out of date but Lord Bathurst thought he should inform Macquarie in a despatch of the dual role of Britain's expedition on behalf of the French Government.

Bathurst's despatch warned "the situation of Port Jackson and Harbour of Sydney hold out vast advantages to its present possessors. Within a few weeks by sail from either the East Indies or Peru, it makes easy trade with both countries profitable. In the case of war its situation would prove of great detriment to Spanish commerce. Captain Baudin expected to see nothing but a few mud huts ... but nothing could exceed his astonishment when he noted ... good buildings everywhere and the expedition observed Sydney with a curious eye."

"The curious eye" of the French also noted the position of the guns around Sydney Cove to protect it from possible attack and the powder magazine in the centre of the barracks. In November 1802, Lesueur was given the services of Lieutenant Boullanger, who had some knowledge of surveying, and they made extensive surveys for one of the most beautiful and detailed maps of Sydney ever produced. The outline has been used for historical reconstruction of Sydney on the front end-paper of this book, and Lesueur's original would doubtless have been of great interest to the French Admiralty. Bathurst also recounted that the defecting French spy had told him of a plan to send four frigates loaded with soldiers to attack and capture Sydney. But Sydney Cove, from the reports of the Baudin and Peron expedition, was thought too difficult to attack. The Cove was under constant surveillance from the Barracks, seen here in Lesueur's drawing on its southern crest and all approaches to the harbour were clearly visible from the South Head, and from the observatory at Dawes Point. Foreign shipping was also visible far out at sea from the tall tower of St. Phillip's Church, just beside the Military or Grosvenor Street windmill, which was also used as an observatory. This square tower is clearly seen on Lesueur's sky-line. The square tower was built in 1797; it started to crumble in June 1799 but was restored. On 4th June, 1806 it was demolished by a storm and the following month the round Norman-style tower of old St. Phillip's was commenced on the site of today's Lang Park.

With all these vantage points duly noted and drawn by Lieutenant Lesueur on either his map or his detailed panorama, the French naval and military authorities must have realised that there was no chance whatever of a surprise attack on Sydney. The French plan was then changed. French soldiers were to land at Broken Bay and attack Parramatta "cutting off the settlers there from Sydney" and also Sydney's supplies of wheat and grain from the farms of Parramatta. The report continued "Parramatta must fall and 1,500 stand of arms are to be delivered into the hands of such convicts who are willing to join the French." By the time Bathurst knew of the invasion plan and had advised Macquarie, the whole danger had long since passed. The

Plate 7 CHARLES ALEXANDRE LESUEUR. **View of Sydney, New Holland in 1802.** *Copper engraving after an original drawing by Lesueur from the Francois Peron Atlas to "Voyage de Decouvertes aux Terres Australes" 1800-1804, first published in Paris in parts from 1807-1816. □ It shows the French camp in the Domain, the first log bridge over the Tank Stream, the original tower of St. Phillip's Church, which was destroyed in a storm, and details of foreign shipping and fortifications required by the French Admiralty for Napoleon's plan to attack Sydney.* Terra Australis.

failure of the Spanish Peninsular Campaign and Napoleon's disastrous loss of soldiers in his retreat from Moscow had made French Imperial expansion to the "Terres Australes" an impossibility. The expedition ended in sadness. Baudin died aboard the *Geographe* and was replaced by de Freycinet. Lesueur, with his drawings and over 2,500 zoological specimens returned to France, where the drawings were "approved" by the Admiralty. Peron spent seven years working on the official account of the voyage and its scientific discoveries.

He died before it was finished and de Freycinet was given the task of completing the mammoth illustrated volumes rather than Lesueur. An embittered Lesueur eventually emigrated to America and, due to the success of his illustrations, was offered the post of Curator of the Museum of Natural Sciences in Philadelphia. He later abandoned this to teach painting to American Indians and, during this period, made many drawings that have a unique place in early American art. His view of Sydney Cove shows tribal Aboriginals, spearing and cooking fish as they had done in the Domain for thousands of years, before the coming of the First Fleet.

Macquarie Street from Campbell's Cove

It is interesting to compare this engraving by Captain Wallis with the identical view painted by Conrad Martens forty years later. They show Sydney changing from a convict settlement guarded by the guns at Dawes Point to a flourishing mercantile city and harbour.

The artist, Captain Wallis, described Sydney under Macquarie as follows: "In the foreground Lieutenant Dawes' Battery commands the Cove, the garden and the stores of Mr Campbell. Government House is in the centre. The surrounding Domain is beautifully situated and commands a view of the Cove and the shipping in it. On the right of Government House are the dwellings of the Governor's Secretary and the Judge-Advocate (David Collins), while in the rear are two fine buildings. The smaller is a Barracks for Cavalry, the larger is the General Hospital. The Government Domain is pleasingly laid out and was planted under the elegant taste of Mrs Macquarie."

Also visible in the Domain was the charming octagonal cottage that the Governor built for Billy Blue, his amusing and eccentric boatman. This little pepper-pot dwelling was the nearest thing to an English Regency folly that Macquarie was allowed to build to ornament his Domain. Billy Blue served the Governor faithfully and made him laugh. There were obviously few others who did this in early Sydney. Poor Lachlan Macquarie was caught between his own dreams of building Sydney into an elegant Georgian town, and the necessity, as a career soldier with his pension to consider, of conforming to the wishes of the Colonial Office to save money.

From the engraving there appear to be four windmills on the eastern ridge, but one is in fact the tip of the Darlinghurst Mill which appears just over the hill. The first two mills were built by John Boston and Commissary John Palmer, the third was Clarkson's Mill at Darlinghurst, while on the extreme right is the post mill built by Henry Kable. Kable began his career as the jailor of the George Street jail but rapidly became one of the Sydney's leading merchants in company with Lord Underwood. The whole partnership eventually split up to the accompaniment of extensive law-suits. But Kable's Mill still survived for many years on the site of today's Public Library of New South Wales, at the corner of Macquarie Street and the Cahill Expressway.

Wallis shows the first buildings of Campbell's warehouse, as well as the side view of Wharf House. Robert and Sophia Campbell returned from London about the time that Wallis made his view of the area.

They found their business faced with financial ruin and debts everywhere. They lived frugally at the once-splendid Wharf House and rented off the wharf and its warehouses in the foreground for a time. Gradually Campbell's hard work and reputation for honesty ensured his return to success.

At the far end of the massive stone warehouse, Wallis shows the large door that guarded the premises against the light-fingered inhabitants of The Rocks. A smaller access door for those living on board the ships alongside the wharf can be seen, so they could come and go at night with a key. The old open sheds were eventually replaced by today's saw-tooth design warehouse, which is now a series of restaurants. Just to the right of Wharf House was the home of Judge Barron Field.

The artist with his sketchbook, talking to the soldier on the right may have been Wallis himself or Joseph Lycett, the convict who was befriended by Wallis, from the days when they both arrived on the same convict transport ship in 1814. Lycett had used his skilled pen to make counterfeit bank notes, when he was short of commissions for his paintings. He was caught and sentenced to 14 years in New South Wales. Wallis took pity on him and found him a job as a clerk in the Police Office. Even close contact with the law did not stop Lycett, who constantly needed money for his addiction to alcohol, turning his hand to more forgery. He was reconvicted and sent as a punishment to the penal settlement at Newcastle.

Wallis by this time had been put in charge of the Newcastle Penal Settlement and once more reprieved Lycett from the chain-gang. He put him to work designing a small church for Newcastle. Lycett's views of New South Wales eventually secured him a pardon from Macquarie and he sailed back to England. However, a pencilled note by an unnamed hand under one of his drawings in the Mitchell Library indicates that he forged still more bank notes and was caught for the third time in England. Threatened again with transportation to Sydney, he committed suicide.

Wallis returned to Sydney in 1819 and advertised sets of his engraved views for sale in the *Sydney Gazette*. These were Australia's first home-produced engravings. The following month he was posted back to London and reprinted his engravings in the book that he wrote describing his period of service in New South Wales.

Plate 8   CAPTAIN JAMES WALLIS. **A View of the Cove and Part of Sydney Taken from Dawes'
Battery.** *Published in his book "An Historical Account of the Colony of New South Wales," London
1821. Mitchell Library. □ Wallis originally published a set of these engravings in Sydney in 1819.
They were engraved by a convict, William Preston, on copper taken from the bottom of a ship, since
this material was in short supply in the colony. They provide some of the most detailed visual records of
Macquarie's Sydney.*

Robert Campbell and Sydney's First Private Wharf

As the youngest son of the Laird of Ashfield, Robert Campbell would have received no income or inheritance from his family estates in the highlands of Scotland. It was quite usual for the younger sons of the Scottish gentry to seek their fortunes in the colonies, since there were few commercial opportunities open to them in Scotland before the industrial revolution. Campbell went to work for a firm of merchants in India, who sent him to Sydney to assess its potential as a suitable trade centre. At that time military officers and government officials controlled all the trade in the colony and sold their own goods for a vast profit to the townsfolk, who had no other option but to pay up or do without the goods.

Campbell immediately saw the commercial potential of Australia, and became the first merchant in Sydney to build his own warehouse and to engage in the export and import trade as a full-time business, rather than a sideline to a military career. Obtaining a lease of waterfront land on the western side of the Cove in 1800, near the site occupied by today's Overseas Passenger Terminal, he built Campbell's Wharf and Warehouse. He maintained and increased his business there for more than forty years. The warehouses were stocked with general household goods, rice and other foods, exotic Cashmere shawls and cottons from India, whale oil, sealskins and cedar and the picture shows their thick stone walls. Seal fur, seal oil and whale oil were then in great demand in England, and Campbell became Australia's major exporter of these goods. He also bought wool from the graziers to add to his export trading.

A man of education, integrity and vision, Campbell appreciated the potential of the infant colony. His interests also ranged from importing sheep and Indian cattle, to horse-breeding and ship-building. His Arabian stud horse, Hector, was the father of much of Australia's first racing blood-stock. Governor King, on his arrival in 1800, described him as "a fair-dealing merchant who by his imports had rescued the settlers and other inhabitants from the oppressive monopolies that have existed here." The people flocked to buy his goods, but the officers of the Rum Corps loathed him for depriving them of their profitable trading side-line although the Corps still kept control of most of the trade in spirits.

Under a contract from Governor King Campbell more than doubled Australia's first cattle herds, bringing in pedigree stock from India that was suited to the arid Australian conditions. But the Rum Corps had long memories, and were to retaliate in a dramatic way during the governorship of William Bligh.

Campbell married one of the prettiest and most accomplished girls in the colony, Sophia Palmer, who had arrived in Sydney in 1800 to stay with her brother and his wife at Woolloomooloo House, from which the present suburb takes its name. Woolloomooloo House was one of the most beautiful homes in Sydney, surrounded by a large farm.

Her portrait shows a girl who looks as if she came from a novel by Jane Austen, complete with Empire neckline, short dark curly hair and piercing blue eyes. Robert Campbell was eight years her senior and the marriage was a long and happy one. It also brought Robert Campbell considerable benefits in trade, since his new brother-in-law as Commissary-General was in charge of all Government contracts for purchasing. Their home, Wharf House, is seen here in Richard Read's panorama. It had a colonnaded verandah and three acres of sloping lawns, where white peacocks and emus roamed at will.

The view from Wharf House was breathtaking. It faced the whole sweep of the Domain and the great spine of the Tarpeian Rock, named in jest after one of the hills of ancient Rome. Facing Campbell's Wharf was the small octagonal cottage that Governor Macquarie built for his favourite boatman, Billy Blue, the extrovert six-foot Jamaican whose constant good humour and ready wit made him laugh. As Australia's first merchant trader and with shrewd Scottish common sense, Campbell picked Sydney Cove's most beautiful site. It also had the advantage of a direct view across to the Flagstaff of the South Head Signal Station, so that Robert Campbell could see his ships returning or sails of overseas shipping that might wish to use the services of his wharf.

On his arrival in 1806 Governor Bligh was told that Campbell "had performed the greatest services to the inhabitants of Sydney, that the price of his merchandise was the same in times of scarcity as it was in abundance." Bligh appointed Campbell Magistrate and Naval Officer in charge of the collection of customs in the port. In that capacity he had to confiscate the illegal spirit stills imported by John Macarthur, which helped to spark off the Rum Rebellion. Its after-effects were to destroy the business which Campbell had built up by hard and honest work.

One night the Palmers, and Robert and Sophia Campbell were dining with Bligh and his daughter at Government House. There must have been many occasions in the future when Robert Campbell regretted his acceptance to dine with the Governor on the evening of 26th January, 1804. For that was the night when George Johnston, as Acting Lieutenant-Governor burst into Government House and placed the Governor under arrest. The Campbells were returned to Wharf House by the soldiers and an armed guard was posted at the door. The family were to be harrassed continually until the arrival of Macquarie.

All the goods going to Campbell's Wharf were rigorously examined but there are legends that Campbell helped a Bligh sympathiser persecuted by the Rum Corps to escape from Sydney and had him nailed up in a barrel and carried on board. However the officers of the Rum Corps were able to revenge old scores with Campbell for taking so much lucrative trade away from their pockets. His ships were delayed by inspections and extra permits, so that they sailed late. When Macquarie arrived, law and order was restored and Campbell's Wharf settled down to normal trading, but this was not for long. As a man of unimpeachable honesty, Campbell was instructed to go to England as a witness for Bligh at the inquiry and possible court-martial of George Johnston. The ship *Hindustan* with Bligh aboard was waiting at this wharf ready to cast off. Poor Robert Campbell who

wᵗʰ at Head of Port   4 Light House.   5 Fort Macquarie.   6 Garden Island.   7 Mr R Campbell's Stores   8 Mr R Campbell's House.   9 Governor's Stables   10 Government House   Guard House

*Plate 9   RICHARD READ, SENIOR. **View of Port Jackson & Part of the Town of Sydney, from a Drawing in the Possession of Barron Field.** Aquatint after an original watercolour, 1820. Mitchell Library. (The key shows Fort Macquarie, Campbell's Warehouse and Wharf House.) □ There were two Richard Reads in Sydney during the Macquarie period. This panorama was painted by Richard Read, Senior, for Judge Barron Field, who succeeded Judge Bent of Bent Street fame, as Chief Judge of the Supreme Court of New South Wales. Read also made a fine watercolour portrait of the grave Judge Field complete with wig and bound volume of poetry.*

had no one to entrust with the management of his business, and feared that it would fail without him, was giving last minute instructions to his clerk when, as he later described, "I received a message from Governor Macquarie by his Secretary that unless I forthwith embarked with my family, he would be under the necessity of sending a file of soldiers to escort me on board."

So the *Hindustan* sailed away from Campbell's Wharf and Campbell's business declined without his supervision as he had feared. He returned to Sydney in March 1815, to find bailiffs in the house, the silver sold to pay off the creditors and his business ledgers full of debtors. Within five years Campbell & Co. were again a great business house in Sydney, due to Robert Campbell's hard work. Through his integrity and vision and his appreciation of the potential of the facilities of the harbour, it became a trading colony rather than purely a convict port.

'The Artful Delinquent' Paints Sydney Cove.

This naive but forceful watercolour is the work of one of Australia's most notorious convicts. John William Lancashire advertised himself in the *Sydney Gazette* as a professional London-trained artist of "experience and knowledge" but since he was one of the greatest rogues, liars and forgers of early Sydney, this claim like many others he made, cannot be taken as strictly truthful.

When sentenced to transportation for seven years he was more accurately described as a draftsman and painter of heraldic crests. He arrived in Sydney on the transport *Barwell* in May 1798, after a voyage where many convicts died of fever and malnutrition. Perhaps the horrors of this voyage influenced Lancashire's subsequent behaviour but, from his arrival in Sydney, he was never out of trouble. One problem of the transportation system was that when pardoned, convicts had to pay their own fare back to England. Possibly Lancashire started out his forgeries with the idea of earning his return passage. But subsequently he became quite prosperous and seemed to have forged his promissory notes out of greed rather than sheer necessity.

Governor King arrived in Sydney in 1800 and found Lancashire in jail awaiting hanging for repeated forgery. King reprieved him with a conditional pardon for subsequent good behaviour due to errors in the legal proceedings made during his trial. King was later to regret this reprieve and to describe Lancashire as an "artful delinquent ... possessed of every cunning that human nature could turn to the worst of purposes."

Two years later Lancashire was again charged with forging bills but, by his own fluent and clever defence, again escaped sentence. However, his unfortunate convict mistress Elizabeth Fielder was jailed for attempting to exchange the forged bills. By 1802 Lancashire had acquired another mistress and his own business as a draftsman and sign writer, painting anything including ships, houses and inn signs from his premises in Chapel Row, now known as Castlereagh Street. Two years later, by 1804, he had prospered sufficiently to buy a cottage with two acres of ground at Brickfield Hill, near today's Railway Station. However he still found it impossible to stay out of trouble, and was accused of having an illicit still on his business premises.

Acquitted for lack of evidence, Lancashire then forged a promissory note in the name of Commissary John Palmer and tried to present it in payment to his butcher. At his trial Lancashire's eloquent defence again nearly saved him. He also complained that although not proven guilty he had been kept in heavy chains in the Essex Street jail. However, Governor King's patience was at an end. Fearing that King would revoke the conditional pardon on his original death sentence, he advertised his cottage for sale in the *Gazette* of March 23rd 1806.

He stowed away on a ship bound for India, but was discovered before the ship departed and sentenced to one hundred lashes and three years' hard labour in Van Diemen's Land. Governor King must have been relieved to deport one of his most troublesome convicts to the much stricter penal settlement of Port Dalrymple, near Launceston.

Lancashire was shipped out of Sydney on the *Venus* and reached Port Dalrymple in June 1806. On the voyage he enlisted the help of one of the female convicts, and through her, persuaded the first mate to join them in a plan to steal the ship. While the ship's captain was ashore delivering despatches from Sydney to the Governor, Lancashire, the first mate and the rest of the convicts seized the ship. They bound and gagged the crew, put them ashore and set sail for New Zealand.

Aboard were precious food supplies, dried goods and building tools intended for the settlements of Port Dalrymple and Hobart. These would have been quite sufficient for Lancashire's party to set up their own small colony on a Pacific Island. Lancashire, his crew and the *Venus*, owned by Robert Campbell, disappeared without trace.

In spite of its lack of perspective, Lancashire's painting remains one of the most detailed records of the first years of Australian settlement. He provides an important view of the stone bridge over the Tank Stream, replacing the first log bridge, built by the marines of the First Fleet in 1788, which had gradually rotted away. The work commenced on the new bridge in mid-1803. By February 1804 the *Gazette* reported that this new stone bridge was nearly finished.

Lancashire's view also shows the Government Wharf, planned by Governor Phillip and designed by Surveyor-General Augustus Alt about 1790. This Government Wharf had just been extended and the great trunks of ironbank which supported it are clearly visible in the painting.

It had a sentry box with a guard, since all the government stores, tools, hardware and provisions were landed here and stored in the large building behind the Wharf, with its four small windows placed high against burglary. This Dry Stores was built in 1791 on the site of the redoubt or look-out platform of the First Fleet. The area behind it was originally known as Dry Stores Row but was later re-named Macquarie Place. From the view it is easy to see how before Circular Quay was built Macquarie Place, with its proximity to the Government Wharf, was the natural administrative commercial centre of Old Sydney Town. It was also close to the waterfront and the offices of the main Government officials. Lancashire shows how The Rocks area developed from groups of cottages, their gardens using any available patch of soil between the rocky ledges. He also shows Old Government House on Bridge Street with its large vegetable garden and boathouses on the wide beach which is now Circular Quay East.

Plate 10 JOHN WILLIAM LANCASHIRE. ***View of Sydney taken from The Rocks.*** *Watercolour signed and dated 1803. Dixson Galleries. □ This primitive watercolour by one of Sydney's most notorious convicts is today one of the most important records of the founding of Australia's first city, and clearly shows the original shape of Sydney Cove and the old stone bridge over the Tank Stream.*

The Rocks
by John Eyre Convict Artist

Plate 11   *JOHN EYRE,* **East View** *(painted from the site of Argyle Street, The Rocks) c.1810. Watercolour. Dixson Library.* □ *Outstanding ability as a topographical artist possibly earned Eyre a remission of his seven-year sentence for burglary, since he was granted a conditional pardon after serving only three years. He stayed in Sydney until 1812, accepting work as a signwriter painting house numbers as well as four different versions of these famous panoramas.*

One set was sent to London for exhibition where it aroused great interest and was reproduced as two pairs of large engravings. Although packed with information, his engravings are curiously stiff. They lack the fluidity of these original watercolours, now badly stained with age. Eyre shows the rocky ledges and steep cliffs that caused this whole area to be named "The Rocks." Convicts had been forced to sleep under these boulders, and violence, drunkenness, robbery and homosexual assault had been nightly occurrences here before Macquarie ordered Greenway to design the Hyde Park Barracks to provide sleeping accommodation for the prisoners. It was to take years of work by the chain-gangs before these rocks were quarried down.

Miller's Point and Darling Harbour
in 1845

Plate 12 GEORGE EDWARD PEACOCK. **Port Jackson, showing the Observatory.** *Oil on canvas. Signed and dated 1845, on a label on the reverse of the painting. Private collection. □ Another educated convict demonstrates the very skills which ensured his transportation for forgery. This is undoubtedly one of Peacock's finest and most important paintings. The silvery, mirror-clear waters of the Harbour reflect the surprising amount of industrial and commercial development that has occurred since Eyre painted it. The wharves and crowded streets of Miller's Point and Darling Harbour contrast sharply with the isolated cottages of the North Shore around Blue's Point. Peacock must have meant Lieutenant Dawes' old Observatory at Dawes Point, since the Sydney Observatory was not built until ten years later. Peacock carefully painted the tall flagstaff, which signalled the arrival of shipping by means of flags to the South Head, where he was assigned as a trusty convict to assist in observing and forecasting the weather from the signal station. The year after he made this magnificent Harbour painting, Peacock received his convict pardon. But, during the severe financial depression of the 1840s, it would have been impossible for him to live entirely by painting and he remained at South Head as government meteorologist. His work there gave him ample time and opportunity to observe the wonderful cloud effects that appear in his paintings.*

Macquarie's Sydney

Plate 13   JOSEPH LYCETT. **North View of Sydney.** *Hand-coloured aquatint from Lycett's "Views in Australia" . . . London 1824. □ On the title page, Lycett coyly describes himself as "Artist to Major-General Macquarie, the late Governor," as though he had been on an official tour of the Colony, rather than shipped out to Sydney in chains aboard a vessel on which one in every nine convicts died. This attractive and sophisticated piece of propaganda for Macquarie's extensive building programme helped to earn Lycett his pardon. Here Fort Macquarie, the Governor's Stables, St. James' Church, the Commissariat Store, the Grosvenor Street or Military Windmill, Fort Phillip and Dawes Observatory are all clearly visible. On the extreme right is the Pyrmont Windmill while inside the old Fort Phillip, site of today's Observatory, flies a gigantic flag. The path worn away by soldiers marching from the military barracks to Fort Phillip eventually was named York Street by Macquarie.*

Photograph courtesy Josef Lebovic Gallery, Paddington.

This elegant view of Sydney Cove in 1822, painted by Joseph Lycett, a convict artist and skilful forger, was also described by Peter Cunningham, Surgeon-Superintendent of Convict Ships when he wrote "Two Years in New South Wales ... the Actual State of Society in that Colony and its peculiar advantages to Emigrants". Cunningham was a surgeon seeking to supplement his income but chose to do so by writing rather than trading like John Boston. His book is one of the most valuable early records of Old Sydney Town.

Cunningham acted as Medical Officer to convicts on their long sea voyage to Sydney. He entered Sydney Cove aboard the convict ships many times and, as an accurate and impartial observer, presented the clearest description of the early town of Sydney that has survived.

His eye-witness account stated "Sydney Cove is formed by two ridges running out into the harbour; the one to the left terminating in Bennelong's Point, on the low extremity where stands Fort Macquarie, with its castellated martello towers; and that to the right, in Dawes Point, with a Fort bearing that name, which in like manner occupies its extremity. Down the hollow between these ridges a small rill trickles slowly into the head of the Cove, in the rocky sandstone bed of which tanks have been cut, to retain the water during the summer droughts ... Along this hollow, for upwards of a mile, extends our main thoroughfare (George Street), which all the other streets either run parallel to or intersect at right angles, the town thus occupying the whole of the hollow, and creeping up the gradual ascents on each side.

"The ridge on the left is successively crowned by the lofty-looking buildings of the Horse Barracks, the Colonial Hospital, the Convict Barracks, and a fine Gothic Catholic Chapel; beyond which lies the promenade of Hyde Park, flanked toward the town by a row of pretty cottages, and toward the country by a high brick-walled garden appertaining to the government. On the ridge to the right of the Cove, rows rising above rows of neat white cottages present themselves, overlooked by the commanding position of Fort Phillip with its Signalpost, flag and telegraphic appendages; following which we behold in succession, the Military Hospital and Windmill; St. James's Church, the Gothic Presbyterian Kirk; and beyond these the Military Barracks, forming three-fourths of a large square and opening to George Street, with an extensive green plot in the centre for purposes of a parade ground. The portion of the town to the right is best known by the name of The Rocks, from the ridge whereon it is built being nothing more than a bare mass of sandstone, often rising in successive layers (like steps of stairs) from the bottom to the top of the ridge. This is considered the St. Giles's, and the division of the town to the left the St. James's, portion of Sydney; most of the superior citizens inhabiting the latter, and the lower classes chiefly the former, though The Rocks can undoubtedly boast many handsome houses with highly respectable inmates.

"A few hundred yards from the head of the Cove, toward the left, stands the Governor's house, with its beautiful Domain in front ... ornamented by large trees of the finest foliage with a fine belt of shrubbery in the background; the whole occupying a space from beyond the head of the Cove to near Bennelong's Point ... But the Domain, beautiful as it still undoubtedly is, has lost much of its attraction since being deprived of the kangaroos and emus seen in Governor Macquarie's time, hopping and frisking playfully about, which never failed to strike powerfully the eye of a stranger on his first sight of them from ship-board, both on account of their novelty to him, and their being emblematical of the country upon whose shore he was about to debark ... You land at the Government Wharf at the right where carts and porters are generally on the lookout for jobs and passing about fifty yards along the avenue, you enter George Street which stretches on both hands. Up to the left you turn to reach the heart of Sydney Town. Near the Harbour, where ground is very valuable, the houses are usually continuous, like those of the towns in England. Generally speaking, the better sort of houses in Sydney are built in the detached cottage style, of white stone, or of brick plastered and whitewashed, one or two storeys high, with verandahs in front, and enclosed by a neat wooden paling, lined occasionally with trim-pruned geranium hedges beside a garden decked with flowers.

The Military Hospital
and the Fort Street School

NATIONAL SCHOOL.

Plate 14
*JOSEPH FOWLES. **The National School.** Engraving from*
his book "Sydney in 1848," showing the alterations made by
colonial architect Mortimer Lewis to the original Macquarie
Military Hospital. Courtesy Mitchell Library.

The site of the Military Hospital was dictated by the need to place it close to the Military Barracks on George Street so that sick soldiers or those who had been flogged nearly to death could be sent to the Military Hospital with the minimum of delay and inconvenience. There were separate quarters for the surgeons at each end of the building, with two large wards to each floor. Double-storey verandahs like this are uncommon in Australia but usual in public and domestic architecture in India and the West Indies, where Watts had previously served with the British Army. In fact Australian architects should be eternally grateful to Watts for importing the concept of the wrap-around double verandah on all sides of a building. This is believed to have been the first building commissioned by Macquarie "the building Governor" in his efforts to provide Sydney with substantial public buildings and good roads. Traces of this old Military Hospital still exist in the National Trust Centre today; for example the imposing front doorway with its 1815 headstone, and several interior walls. With the establishment of the Victoria Barracks at Paddington in the 1840s, the Military Hospital was no longer needed on Observatory Hill. It was closed in 1848 and the building was transferred to the newly-established Board of Education for use as the Model or National School.

The building was enlarged and elaborated with heavy arches around the verandahs and lattice work inserts by colonial architect Mortimer Lewis. Joseph Fowles described the Model School as "intended for the preparation of efficient teachers with whom the various district schools of the Colony will be supplied and who, upon completion of their education, will have diplomas granted to them. The teachers who taught the Australian teachers were imported from the Model National School in Ireland." Eventually it became the Fort Street School. For years the building smelt of slates and sandwiches and chalk. The boys wore knickerbockers and played marbles, the girls wore demure pinafores and long braids. Discipline was severe, but many eminent Sydney men and women owe their education to the old Fort Street School.

Today the National Trust Centre's beautiful Ervin Gallery commemorates a remarkable Australian. Harry Ervin grew up in Mosman, and as a young man was fascinated by artists like Arthur Streeton and Tom Roberts who camped and painted at Sirius Cove. He bought their paintings and became their friend. Harry Ervin became a wool buyer for an overseas firm and on his death 1977 donated a very substantial sum to assist the National Trust to both purchase and exhibit Australian works of art on the site of Watts and Macquarie's Military Hospital. Sadly he never lived to see the magnificent conversion that he had helped to fund.

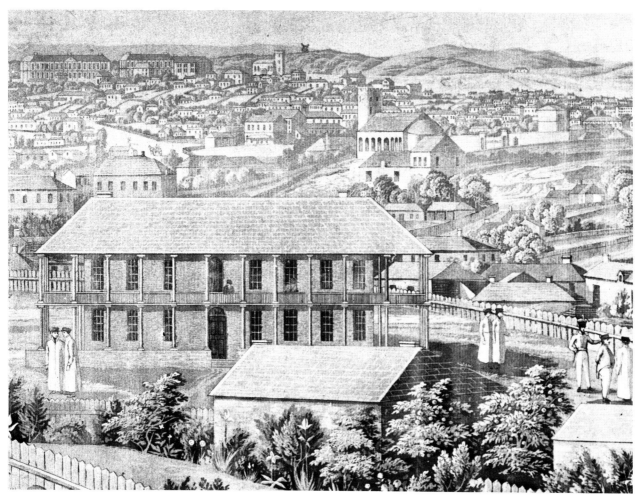

Plate 15 MAJOR JAMES TAYLOR. *c. 1820-1822. Detail from his engraved aquatint entitled* **The Town of Sydney** *showing Macquarie's Military Hospital, which now forms part of the headquarters of the National Trust of New South Wales and the S. H. Ervin Gallery. Mitchell Library, Sydney.* □ *Major Taylor remained in Sydney for only six years. When he lived there it had a population of some 16,000 convicts, approximately 14,000 ex-convicts, and half that number of free settlers and military. His enormous panorama of the entire town was designed to give the English an idea of the development of their new colony overseas. In the foreground he showed the Military Hospital, recently built by order of Governor Macquarie from designs by his talented aide-de-camp, Lieutenant John Watts. The building was completed in 1815 and designed "for the accommodation of one hundred patients." Watts had trained as an architect in Ireland before enlisting in the Army during the Napoleonic Wars.*

Today the building is situated close to the Observatory and the southern approaches to Harbour Bridge, but then it was surrounded by green fields and flowers. Major Taylor drew the convalescent soldiers roaming about in its gardens in long nightshirts. To conform with current picturesque conventions they look more like mediaeval Doges in Venice than sick sergeants. Just behind the Military Hospital can be seen the first church of St. Phillips called after the Governor, not "Philip" after the Saint. This church was consecrated by the Rev. Samuel Marsden in December 1810, with a little round Norman tower which replaced the large square tower that fell down in a storm. The convicts were forced to attend services there and they hated it, but it gave its name to Church Hill.

The Taverns of the Rocks

Plate 16 *AUGUSTUS EARLE.* **Natives of New South Wales.** *Lithograph published 1830. (Detail)*

Plate 17 *GEORGE ROBERTS. Detail from* **The Punchbowl, Gloucester Street, The Rocks in 1845.** *Pencil drawing. Dixson Library, Sydney.*

As Sydney grew and its trade prospered, taverns, brothels and sly-grog shops sprang up around The Rocks and Miller's Point to cater for the needs of visiting seamen from all parts of the globe.

In Macquarie's Sydney, with a population of just over 10,000 people, more than 100 grog licences were issued annually by the government, while the illegal grog shops advertised their presence by a striped red and white pole placed discreetly outside. Every night men flocked to these areas for rum and women. For many ex-convicts and convicts, living without their families, rum was the only diversion. The clientele of the pubs was swelled by the wealthy crews from the whaling ships, who arrived with several months' wages in their pockets to spend. Seafarers from all over the Pacific had heard of the notorious Rocks, with its tangle of hilly lanes and steps and tumble-down cottages.

The noise of revelry and snatches of drunken song was supposed to be heard at sea for a mile on a calm night. There were others who said that the smell from its insanitary back street hovels carried nearly as far!

The ex-convicts who ran the taverns perhaps unconsciously recreated the atmosphere of the back streets of their native towns in England. The Rocks was lavishly endowed with pubs with traditional names like The Lord Nelson, The Hero of Waterloo, The Cat and Fiddle and The Black Dog. Some of the pubs even looked as though they were in Merry England. The Punchbowl in Gloucester Street, seen here, could be part of a Cornish or Scottish fishing village. With its low white-washed walls and tiny latticed windows it suggested roaring log fires and cosy oak settles rather than convicts sodden with rum and harlots for hire, as described in the eye-witness accounts of some visitors to The Rocks.

Augustus Earle's lithograph shows some Aboriginals drinking a highly intoxicating spirit known as bull, made from fermented sugar bags soaked in a bucket of water. The tavern behind them with its colonnaded balcony and kangaroo inn-sign looks uniquely Australian. Drunken convicts and ladies of the town carouse around its doorway. To judge from contemporary accounts of Sydney Town, no population on the face of the earth ever absorbed more alcohol per head of population than Sydney. No business transaction was deemed complete without a "nobbler" of rum and so possibly began the unique Australian custom of "shouting" a round of drinks in the pub.

In 1847 Alexander Harris described clearly the beginnings of the Australian sense of "mateship" and independence, when he visited the tap-room of a Sydney pub where "almost everybody was drinking rum in drams. One remarkable peculiarity in common to them all was that ... every man seemed to consider himself on a level with all the rest.

Plate 18 JOHN RAE. **The oldest pub in Sydney, The Hero of Waterloo, Miller's Point in 1842.**
Watercolour from the Dixson Gallery.

The dudeen, or clay pipe, was in everybody's mouth. I think there was not an individual in the room who did not smoke ... and not a shin in the room had either stocking or sock." The great classic description of The Rocks in the 1860s describes it as "the land of fiddlers and brazen hussies, of rum and eternal spree, where nightly occur dancing, sing-ing, brawling, curses and coarse revelry. Here are narrow, murky lanes, dirty women and children and loafing, unshaven, drunken men."

John Rae's watercolour shows two of Sydney's most colourful taverns. First was the Whaler's Arms, named for its clientele, whose ships can be seen moored at Miller's Point in John Rae's watercolour. The men from these ships sometimes spent two months' wages in two nights ashore in the taverns.

At the junction of Lower Fort Street and Windmill Street, Rae showed The Hero of Waterloo, the oldest Sydney tavern still in existence.

Its facade has scarcely changed today but it had a very grim reputa-tion for its stone cellars, where unruly drunks were locked up to await the arrival of the police to take them to the jail. There is a ghastly legend that several publicans in The Rocks, instead of handing over the unconscious bodies in their cellars to the police, sold them off for a good price to unscrupulous sea-captains who were short of crew just before departure. When the alcoholic reveller finally came to he found himself far out to sea on a totally different ship and had to work his passage as one of the crew to his new destination.

Miller's Point
and the Last Windmill

Plate 19 *JOHN SKINNER PROUT.* **Miller's Point from the Flagstaff (now Observatory Hill).**
Lithograph from "Sydney Illustrated" by J. S. Prout and J. Rae, published 1842. Courtesy Josef
Lebovic Gallery, Paddington.

*Plate 20   SAMUEL ELYARD. **Miller's Point Windmill.** Undated watercolour from the artist's sketchbook. Dixson Galleries.*

flags. Different colours and symbols were used on the second flagstaff to announce to Sydney's population that the longed-for ships had arrived, bringing letters from relatives in the old country.

Courting couples met at the flagstaff, nursemaids walked their young charges there and hoped to meet a handsome young soldier and, as usual in early Sydney, the goats were everywhere. The Lord Nelson Inn remains today, an old tavern of charm and character.

Rae described the windmill in the background as "belonging to a Mr Davis, who bequeathed it to the Roman Catholic Church, with a view to erecting a nunnery." It was never built. Perhaps the Church decided that Miller's Point with its seamen's taverns, sly grog shops and houses of ill-fame was not exactly suitable for a nunnery.

The area was originally known as Cockle Bay Point. Some believe that the name was changed in honour of the original miller, named Jack Leighton or Jack-the-Miller, others that it was named by Governor Phillip to honour his private secretary, Andrew Miller, also the first Commissary-General.

Samuel Elyard delighted in painting "the rustic, the makeshift and the decrepid" and he loved the old tumble-down Sydney windmills. He did not state which of the three mills at Miller's Point this was, but from its location close to the water, it is most likely that it was the mill Rae described as "built immediately under Albion House", the strange three-storey building to the left of Davis's Mill. Albion House was then a cheap lodging house, known locally as "The Pack of Cards", since it looked in imminent danger of collapsing into Darling Harbour.

Jack Leighton may have been a good miller, but he was a poor judge of real estate. He turned down a free offer to become the owner of the whole of Miller's Point because the terms of the land grant would have required him to spend a few pounds and fence in the whole area. He had a quick but dramatic death when he fell off the rickety ladder of his old post-mill after a few too many drinks.

At one time Sydney had nineteen windmills to grind its flour. They must have been an amazing sight to foreign ships approaching Sydney Cove, as they whirled and creaked on their great towers.

*Plate 20a   SAMUEL ELYARD. **Old Windmill, South Head Road.** 1868. Dixson Galleries.*

Prout migrated to Sydney from England in 1840, believing that he would earn enough from his paintings to support his wife and ten children. He soon found this was impossible since Martens obtained most of the important commissions. So he lectured on painting, gave lessons and went into the field of publishing. He teamed up with John Rae, a keen amateur artist who may have been his pupil. Together they compiled and published a book of Prout's Sydney sketches with descriptive text by Rae, the well-informed town clerk. Under this lithograph Rae wrote "This view is taken from Fort Phillip Hill, a little to the south-west of the Flagstaff."

Prout drew the simple stone cottages of Miller's Point, unadorned by iron lace or verandahs, which were then inhabited by sailors, wharfies, boat builders and self-employed artisans. There were in fact two enormous flagstaffs, braced by heavy chains against the winds. They stood beside the crumbling ramparts of Fort Phillip, which was soon to be replaced by the Sydney Observatory. "One corresponded telegraphically with the flagstaff at South Head, while the other was for the benefit of the inhabitants of Sydney." Messages passed between South Head and Flagstaff Hill by a series of colour-coded

Old Sydney Streets

Plate 21   H. STUART WILSON. **Cumberland Street c. 1880.** *Signed oil from the collection of the Mitchell Library, showing the decaying mansion 'Cumberland House', once the home of wealthy Joseph Moore, from whose wharf at Miller's Point the first gold shipment from Australia was sent to London.* □ *Although the Bunker's Hill end of Cumberland Street was once flanked by the elegant Georgian homes of wealthy merchants, much of the street became a narrow alley winding between decaying cottages and terrace homes. Often the road was roughly hacked out along the hill contours, leaving many of the dwellings perched high above the street level, approached by the sort of rough steps seen here. Sanitation was poor and drinking water was either purchased by the bucket or obtained from wells dug in the rocky outcrop. Children, chickens and goats all played together in the kerbless gutters. Cumberland Street had a royal title, it was named by Governor Macquarie after the King's son, the eccentric Duke of Cumberland. After the great plague clean-up of The Rocks, when many of its hovels were razed to the ground, its name was changed to York Street North but it was recently returned to the original name of Cumberland Street given by Macquarie, much to the confusion of local inhabitants, who are continually asked where is that new street called Cumberland Street.*

Goats roamed everywhere in The Rocks in the early days. Colonel Mundy commented that "that picturesque animal the goat forms a conspicuous item of the Sydney street menagerie, amounting to a pest little less dire than a plague of dogs."

Plate 22

SAMUEL ELYARD. **(Clyde Street), Miller's Point.** *From a folio of the artist's sketches in the Dixson Galleries, Sydney.* □ *Elyard loved to paint the winding lanes and waterfront areas of The Rocks and Miller's Point. It is not surprising that Clyde Street resembled a picturesque Scottish fishing village with its stone cottages and McAusland's General Store on the corner. It was originally built by Dr Dunmore Lang's "virtuous Protestant artisans." By his lecture tours in Scotland, Dr Lang had encouraged many skilled Scottish ship-builders and mechanics to emigrate to Australia. Surrounded on all sides by the Catholic Irish of Miller's Point, they had turned Clyde Street into a virtual Scottish ghetto.*

This is one of the most delightful of Elyard's watercolours. The steeply-pitched roofs, overhanging balconies and glimpse of the sailing boats all add interest to the scene, and the figures of the lady gathering up her shopping basket and the chimney sweep in his top hat provide human interest in the foreground. It is unlikely that Elyard made this painting for sale, since there would have been little money to spare for pictures in Miller's Point. He did exhibit some of his best watercolours and in common with Martens, Frederick Terry and George French Angas was chosen to represent Australian art at the Paris International Exhibition in 1867.

Samuel Elyard
and the Queens Wharf

Samuel Elyard was one of the most prolific painters of early Sydney. Born in England, he arrived there as a young child in 1821, aboard the convict transport on which his father was Surgeon-Superintendent. Up to 1823 the family lived at the Carter Barracks, where his father, Dr William Elyard, was Medical Superintendent of convicts until Samuel was six years old. His father had received substantial land grants during his term of government service and Samuel Elyard's home background was prosperous, cultured and stable.

He showed great aptitude for painting while at school in Sydney and became acquainted with Conrad Martens, whose portrait he painted. Martens encouraged the enthusiastic young artist, but advised him to concentrate on landscapes rather than portraits. "I paint the beautiful scenes of nature," he explained to the young man, "and have a life of delight, but you will have to paint people's faces which are often ugly, silly or vicious in appearance, and therefore can give you no pleasure."

Elyard purchased several watercolours from Martens and realised that, when an artist as talented as Martens had difficulty supporting himself by painting, he himself would do better to continue as a week-end painter.

Accordingly he took a job as clerk in the Colonial Secretary's Office and spent some of his spare time taking lessons in landscape painting from John Skinner Prout. He painted with an obsessional fervour, rapidly and with great fluency and some of his early paintings such as those of Craignathan or Miller's Point have been sadly underestimated. However the importance of his work has recently been recognised by being accorded a travelling exhibition around New South Wales, sponsored by the Regional Galleries Association. From Jonathan Watkin's detailed research for this exhibition many new aspects of Elyard's complex life have emerged.

Elyard's importance today is as a topographical painter with an unusually wide choice of subjects for his period. With a secure public service position and family money behind him he was one of the few artists who were free to paint the Sydney scenes that interested him, rather than choosing standard views of the harbour and the Domain and the homes of the wealthy. In his journal he wrote that he loved to paint "the old, the rustic or the makeshift," and scenes like Sydney's windmills, wharves and winding lanes were to be recurrent themes throughout his long career. The more decayed and picturesque they were, the more he enjoyed painting them. Although Elyard found comfort and mental stimulation from his painting, by the late 1840s, he was diagnosed by his doctor as morbidly depressed, highly anxious and obsessional. During this period he was unfortunate enough to meet the lady who was to insinuate herself into his life "like a serpent," as he recalled during a written appeal to the Church for a annulment of his marriage.

Mrs Angelina Hallet was a woman of mystery. Although she announced that she was widowed, Mr Hallett may even have been alive when she went through some type of marriage ceremony with the confused and depressed artist. He stated afterwards that she convinced the Elyard family to dispense with their own doctor explaining that his medical treatment was actually making poor Samuel worse.

Instead she nursed him, providing her own medicine and Elyard believed that "some drug may have been mixed by her with it, for I acted as I do not think I should have done if my head had been perfectly clear." What he did, under the influence of her 'medicine' was to marry her and it proved a disaster, the effects of which were to haunt him for many years. Still more 'medicine' which may have been laced with belladonna, kept him in the state of constant excitement so feared by the Elyard family.

She tried to persuade him to place his family property into her own name and threatened to commit him to a lunatic asylum in a strait jacket when he refused. But now his family were intensely worried, and after careful investigations, Elyard's brother, William, was able to expose Mrs Angelina Hallett as a former prostitute and petty thief, rather than the respectable widow she had claimed to be. Angelina left the house and Elyard's life, but the combination of her 'medicine' and the stress of the whole relationship had unbalanced the artist into a confused and schizophrenic condition from which he was to suffer intermittently for the next twenty years.

The dissolution of this unusual marriage provided Sydney with a scandal that embraced even the Governor, when Angelina claimed that she was FitzRoy's mistress. There was already a great deal of scandal regarding the amours of the widowed FitzRoy. Although Angelina Hallett was a confirmed liar, there may have been some truth in the story since, when imprisoned for petty theft and child stealing, she was released by special order of Governor FitzRoy.

After her departure Elyard's obsessions centred around the confusion in his mind between his own name of Elyard and that of the Old Testament prophet Elias or Elijah. He had privately printed a series of posters demanding his own recognition as that Biblical prophet, often signing himself as "Elias" or "Samuel Elyard, Emperor of Australia." He donated money to the Sydney synagogue in the name of "Elias" and must have spoken with some conviction, since the recently appointed rabbi of the synagogue, Herman Hoelzel actually signed his name to a petition in the name of "Samuel Elyard (Elias), High Priest of the Jews," demanding Elyard's right to preach in all churches throughout Australia. The president of the synagogue was shown the petition, another scandal erupted and in 1858 Hoelzel was forced to resign for supporting such an amazingly ludicrous cause, and had to return to England in disgrace.

Elyard then turned his obsessional energy back to his painting. By 1868 he was painting so much that he was advised to his doctor to "avoid painting and everything connected with it for a week at a time or his dangerous nerve fever would increase." In 1869 he was forced to resign from the Colonial Secretary's Office due to "ill-health". He left the city he had spent so many years painting and settled on land owned by the Elyard family at Nowra. The move to rustic tranquillity coupled with the avoidance of stress and the loving care of his family gradually effected a cure. His delusions slowly lifted and he settled into a calm old age, painting and photographing windmills and cottages in his own picturesque style. He died in 1910, having established a high reputation as a pioneer of landscape photography and his obituary described him as "a noted painter, well known and highly esteemed."

The Charm of the Rocks

*Plate 24   JOHN HARDWICK. **Princes Street in 1853.** Pencil sketch. Mitchell Library.*

Princes Street was originally known as Windmill Row when, in 1808, it was granted by Acting-Governor George Johnston to his friend John Macarthur. Johnston's land grant could not be ratified until the arrival of Macquarie, who, in 1810, changed its name from *Windmill Row* to the more elegant *Prince* later *Princes Street* after the Prince of Wales. At that time the street was a straggle of wooden convict huts, many still without glass in their windows. However, their superb views over the harbour gradually attracted respectable artisans, boat-builders, sail-makers and ships' captains, who rebuilt or improved the cottages and added verandahs, picket fences and front gardens gay with geraniums. From the rear windows the captains' wives could see the flags on the Signal Station at South Head announcing the arrival of a ship, which could mean the safe return of their husbands. Five years after Hardwick made his drawing, William Jevons of the Royal Mint described Princes Street as "presenting a pleasing and ordered appearance, with the exception of a few small dirty cottages, the remnants of convict times," while Hardwick noted at the bottom of his drawing "These

houses give a good idea of the verandah style of architecture in vogue here."

On the far right is a handsome row of terrace houses complete with first-floor verandahs and French windows, while on the extreme left in front of the horse and cart is one of Jevons' "sagging, tumble-down, little wooden cottage from convict days." Princes Street looked out over the masts of the sailing ships anchored off The Rocks, to Government House and the harbour. It ran past the old Military Hospital down to Dawes Point and lay between Kent and Cumberland Streets. The tiny panes of the Georgian sash windows provided some privacy for the cottages' front parlours and Princes Street had some of the unique charm of a Cornish fishing village. It was unfortunate that it lay right under the approaches to the new Harbour Bridge and these gingerbread Georgian cottages were gradually demolished around 1927 to build the Bradfield Highway. Had it survived, Princes Street would undoubtedly have rivalled neighbouring Argyle Place as a picturesque Sydney tourist attraction today.

34

Plate 25 FREDERICK CHARLES TERRY. **Argyle Place and the Garrison Church from Observatory Hill.** *Watercolour, signed and dated 1850. Mitchell Library.* □ *In 1810 Governor Macquarie named Argyle Place after the town of his birth in Scotland. Over the years it has changed from a residence of ex-convict pimps, robbers, wharf labourers, boat-builders and seafarers into one of Sydney's most peaceful areas, with the charm of an English village green. Now one of the show-places of Australia, there are over twenty different designs of iron lace preserved in the delicate balustrades and friezes of its early homes. Surprisingly the houses look more elegant today, with their pastel colours and white iron lace, than they did then. Terry provides a glimpse of life at The Rocks with his Chinese vegetable sellers, their wares slung from a bamboo pole, the children playing games and the men propped against the fence, loafing in the sun.*

On the far right is the Garrison Church, the second oldest in the city which was built in 1840 to take the overflow of soldiers from St. Phillip's on Church Hill. The first service was held in 1843, in the church designed by Henry Ginn, when the pews overflowed with redcoats eager to see the new church. It may have disappointed them since it was a fairly basic building, its windows made out of oiled canvas. The church was enlarged and made considerably more elegant by Edmund Blacket, and to match Blacket's architecture the mother of David Scott Mitchell donated the church's first stained glass windows. In front of the church stands an elegant private carriage while playful dogs scamper behind. Both Terry and Gill must have loved dogs, as one or two seem to appear in all their drawings, sometimes in totally unexpected places.

Plate 26

CONRAD MARTENS. **Campbell's Wharf, Circular Quay in 1855.** *(Detail) Signed and dated watercolour from the collection of the National Trust of Australia (New South Wales), S. H. Ervin Art Gallery, reproduced here and on the cover by kind permission of the Trust. □ Undoubtedly one of Martens' finest watercolours, this painting has recently returned to Australia after a long residence in England. Its luminous colouring and interesting diagonal composition heighten the interest of the viewer, which is entirely fitting for an important painting of one of Australia's most historic areas. From Dawes Point, the artist looks across Robert Campbell's wharf and warehouses to Circular Quay, literally the cradle of Australia.*

Sir William Dixson much admired this painting and published it as an illustration to his "Notes on Australian Artists" in the Journal of the Royal Australian Historical Society. He noted that the building at the top of the hill on the right was the Miles Building, erected in 1842. The ship lying off Campbell's Wharf was the 'Lady Blackwood', whose captain, John Dibbs, was the father of Sir George Dibbs, who subsequently became a Premier of New South Wales.

Plate 27   (SIR WILLIAM) ELLIOT JOHNSON attrib. **Argyle Cut, Sydney.** Oil on board. National Library of Australia. The painting is signed Elliott Johnstone. □ In 1843 when General Barney was carrying out his reclamation of the muddy foreshores of the harbour, his most pressing need was for rubble and dressed stone to create the massive sea wall of Circular Quay. To provide this it was decided to act on previous proposals and cut away the rocky ridge that divided the two parts of Argyle Street. Work was commenced by convict labour. With pick-axes and shovels they hewed their way through the solid spine of The Rocks, so the bullock waggons could haul their loads through the Cut, connecting the now flourishing area of Darling Harbour with Circular Quay. The Cut is still used as the main east-west thoroughfare through The Rocks.

Building the Argyle Cut

Plate 28   *F. C. TERRY. **Building the Argyle Cut.***
Steel engraving dated 1853. Private collection.

On 5th August, 1804 the *Sydney Gazette* complained bitterly about the access to Miller's Point from The Rocks to Darling Harbour. George Howe, who printed the *Sydney Gazette*, lived near the junction of George Street North and Globe Street at this time. Perhaps he was so tired of the lack of streets running from east to west that he printed the following item in the *Gazette*, saying "It is rather a matter of surprise that a quarter of the town as thoroughly peopled as The Rocks should be without a safe or indeed any central avenue. From the lack of this communication any people who reside in the Back Rows or The High Street (George Street North) or between there and the Hospital Wharf must necessarily take a circuit by way of the New Windmill ... This, like all other undertakings by which the Public are to benefit would certainly be generally supported by means of subscription were the plan agitated for."

This appeal failed to awaken the Governor to the urgent necessity for a thoroughfare for the inhabitants of The Rocks. The next suggestion was put by Alexander Berry of Berry's Bay. He suggested forming an "Argyle Street Company ... to levy a toll on all persons, horses, cattle and carriages passing through the Cut. A penny to be levied on every four-legged animal, horse, bull, ox or cow." Dogs and goats were not excluded and carts were twopence extra. But nothing was done until 1843 when the convict chain-gangs, in their yellow and grey suits, descended from the Hyde Park Barracks to dig through the massive rock walls shown in Elliot Johnson's painting. In spite of the fear of a flogging if they failed to fulfil their day's work quota, by the following year they had only cut between Cumberland and Gloucester Streets. After transportation to Australia was ended there was a halt to work for some time.

The work was finally completed with the help of explosives and free labour in 1859. Overhead bridges were cut for Gloucester Street in 1862, Cumberland Street in 1864 and the Princes Street in 1867-1868. Terry's picture shows the interesting method by which they constructed these bridges.

The Rocks by Sir William Elliot Johnson
Painter and Politician

These two pencil drawings were made by a remarkable Australian whose career advanced from scenery painter at Covent Garden, to merchant seaman and parliamentarian. He was also a freedom fighter in South America, Speaker of the House of Representatives in Canberra, and official representative of the Australian Parliament at the Coronation of George V at Westminster. He was born in poverty in 1862 in Newcastle-upon-Tyne and his parents separated while he was still a boy. Aged only thirteen, he ran away from home to join his father, John Johnson, who was a painter of scenery at the Covent Garden Opera House. His father encouraged his natural talent for painting and this theatrical quality is apparent in works such as his oil of the Argyle Cut, reproduced on Page 38.

In search of adventure he joined the merchant navy and rose to the rank of second mate. He jumped ship at New York and worked there briefly as a scenic artist before making his way overland to South America. He became a freedom fighter in the civil war between Chile and Peru, but as a paid mercenary rather than from revolutionary idealism. In later life he hinted that although only twenty, he had been in command of a guerilla brigade of freedom fighters.

He arrived at The Rocks as second mate on a ship in 1883 when he was only 21. He may have stayed in one of the many seaman's hostels or private lodging houses of the area at this period, because he made numerous signed sketches of The Rocks and Kent Street then. He was fascinated by its winding lanes and steep steps. Possibly the narrow stone terraces reminded him of the back lanes of the port of Newcastle-upon-Tyne of his childhood. Elliot Johnson's drawings are always full of human interest. Shawl-clad women chat in doorways while a Chinese vegetable seller with his long pigtail sells vegetables from door to door at Hart's Stairs, Essex Street. In Trinity Avenue working-men plod wearily home with their shovels over their shoulders while a young girl sweeps the steps and a lass in her best dress walks out with a sailor. Trinity Avenue connects Argyle Street and Lower Fort Street and the artist shows one of the typical streets of The Rocks hacked out of the stone, so characteristic of the whole area.

However, the former merchant seaman soon moved away from The Rocks and began a highly successful new life in his adopted country. He won the Liberal seat of Lang, New South Wales in the Federal Parliament and rose to become Speaker of the House between 1913-1914 and 1917-1923. He was knighted for his services in 1920 and died twelve years later, having lived the classic rags-to-riches story. Even at the end of his life he still continued to paint the Australian scenes that interested him, showing his characteristic inclusion of a wealth of social detail.

He took a great deal of interest in the selection of the site for the Federal Capital, nominated the Yass-Canberra site which was eventually chosen, and made some of the first drawings of Australia's new capital city. He was known as a tenacious speaker in the House and as a most amusing performer at dinner functions, when he would often provide colourful accounts of his voyage around Cape Horn. He would recount tales of the days when all hands caught scurvy and of the shipwrecks that he survived and his guerilla war experiences. *The Australian Magazine* described his parliamentary career as "gifted with a tenacity of purpose which enables him to hold the floor of the Legislative Assembly fearlessly in the presence of his opponents and to talk them to death."

Arriving as a merchant seaman in the 1880s, Elliot Johnson saw two widely differing views of life in Australia. As well as the charm of The Rocks with its winding lanes, harbour views, and steep stairs, he saw the tougher side of Sydney where these same lanes by night were ideal for robbing and waylaying the unwary seamen who drank in the taverns. The age-old trick of the world's sea ports was often played out along these narrow streets. Seen under a dim street light a girl appearing full of allure would beckon the sailor into a dark lane-way like the infamous Suez Canal, where her male protectors would rob the poor unfortunate of his money and leave him half dead. Cambridge Street, Little Essex Street and Harts Stairs itself were often favoured by the muggers of The Rocks. William Stanley Jevons, an Assayer at the Royal Mint was particularly interested in The Rocks when he made his famous "Social Survey of Sydney" and his description aptly complements some of the early drawings of Sir William Elliot Johnson. William Jevons described how "Essex Street, Essex Lane, Brown Bear Lane (which led down from Harts Stairs), and Globe Street are all streets, not roads, being scarcely traversable by vehicles and destitute of all signs of metalling, guttering or sewering. The houses which line them are small and comparatively ancient stone cottages, so unevenly and irregularly built that the doorstep of one residence sometimes approximates to the roof and eaves of another. The interior of these abodes usually consists of two dirty bare chambers of small size, yet too large for the scanty articles which constitute their furniture ... But what chiefly requires remedy is the utter absence of all means of drainage, which subsequently lies where it is and poisons the ground beneath and the air above ... Again in many cases the front or back of a house or a whole row of houses stand close to a wall of rock, upon the summit of which are erected the privies of the next higher row of houses, while various channels discharge incessant streams of drainage."

late 29 SIR WILLIAM ELLIOT JOHNSON. **Trinity Avenue, The Rocks.** □ *Detail from a signed pencil drawing showing the steps leading from Trinity Avenue up to the more elegant Bunker's Hill area, with its solid Georgian stone homes built for sea captains, merchants and Colonial officials. National Library of Australia.*

Plate 30
SIR WILLIAM ELLIOT JOHNSON. **Harts Stairs, (Little) Essex Street.** □ *Signed pencil drawing showing the typical stone terraces of The Rocks. In the background along Gloucester Street is the notorious Ocean Wave Hotel. It was originally known as The Black Dog and built by the wealthy ex-convict Samuel Terry, sometimes called "The Botany Bay Baron." From its overhanging balcony the fiery Dr Dunmore Lang once held a public meeting, haranguing the assembled crowds below on the evils of convict transportation. This whole area changed dramatically after the 1900 plague epidemic and many of these narrow lanes were destroyed in the resulting clean-up of The Rocks. National Library of Australia.*

Crime and Punishment
in George Street

In 1788 one of Governor Phillip's most pressing problems was where to jail convicts who committed further crimes in Sydney. The convicts constantly stole food and clothing from each other and from the officials and marines. There was no jail and, until one could be built, confining them in a tent was an unsatisfactory solution. So until the jail was built they were shipped off to Pinchgut Island, now Fort Dennison.

The name of Pinchgut was given to the island by marooned convicts whose ration of bread and water was rowed over to them once a week. The first George Street Jail was built of logs and burnt down in 1799, when barely two years old. Arson was suspected but never proved and a more substantial building was obviously required. The number of absconding assigned convict servants was increasing and a site where they could be flogged was necessary. Assigned servants were also punished by imprisonment for laziness, drunkenness, and theft.

The cost of building and materials was paid for by the customs dues, which were to be levied by the naval officer, Surgeon William Balmain. The stone jail was completed at the end of 1800 and was surrounded by the high stone wall shown by de Sainson. It also appears from the waterfront in the panoramas of George William Evans and John Eyre, with the same arched doorway to the rear.

In 1822 Commissioner Bigge inspected the George Street Jail and it achieved the dubious distinction of being one of the only sites in Sydney where he advised that more money should be spent. He found the security of the jail so poor that the majority of convicts needed to be kept in chains. There were only two small cells for male prisoners, and hardened criminals, debtors, those awaiting trial and important witnesses were all locked up together. The innocent were held in irons along with the guilty, and the women and children were confined together. Bigge commissioned Greenway to choose a site for a new jail and Greenway designed another jail for Darlinghurst, where there was a plentiful supply of sandstone. However Greenway was dismissed from his post and Mortimer Lewis, the newly appointed colonial architect, refused to work with Greenway's plans.

Meanwhile conditions at the old jail became worse. Drainage and disease were a constant problem. It was here that Private Sudds died of fever after being imprisoned by Governor Darling for trying to avoid service with his regiment, which was to be posted to India. He committed petty larceny so that he would be dismissed from the Army and as an example to other soldiers Major-General Darling decided to imprison him as a civilian. He was weighed down with heavy leg irons linked by chains and made to wear a spiked iron collar around his neck until the day before his death. The resulting scandal forced Darling's resignation as Governor.

Behind the demure wall with its arched gate, the jail was a place of horrors. Condemned convicts were guarded here in chains until they were taken out to be hanged as a public spectacle, watched by a jeering crowd. Originally the alleyway by the jail was named Middlesex Lane but when it was widened it received the name of Essex Street. After 1820 it was always known as Gallows Hill from the gibbet which hung there. To avoid the danger of a public riot, the gallows was moved inside the prison walls and the crowds used to gather on the ridge of The Rocks to the west to watch the gruesome spectacle below them.

By the 1830s, space was at such a premium that even the solitary confinement cell was often used to accommodate three prisoners, for lack of other space.

Today, in one of the supreme ironies of fate, the stones of the old George Street Jail have become part of the foundations of one of Australia's finest hotels. Few of the guests who pay to be pampered in luxury realise that a building on the same site once offered free accommodation at His Majesty's pleasure. Instead of air-conditioned suites with harbour views, the convicts had a reeking and overcrowded cell furnished with a rusty bucket for sanitation, and one pump provided washing and drinking facilities for nearly 300 prisoners. Today an elegant restaurant in the Regent Hotel commemorates that remarkable man, Henry Kable, who ran the first stage coach to Parramatta, founded a dynasty, and acted as the first jailor. But the rations he was required to give the prisoners were scarcely a la carte fare, since they consisted of nothing but a pound of bread a day for each prisoner.

Despite horrified despatches to London from each successive new Governor, Sydney's own version of "The Black Hole of Calcutta" continued to operate on George Street until 1841. Then convicts, shivering and miserable in clanking irons, guarded by armed police and warders, shambled along George Street from the old prison to the new. Some 119 men and boys with a convicted murderer in a van at the rear, heavily weighed down with irons, shuffled past the watching crowds. Then came the slow sad spectacle of thirty-nine women, unkempt, hollow-eyed with fatigue and in chains. This small procession ensured Darlinghurst Jail was populated and prices of real estate rose along George Street.

Plate 31   LOUIS DE SAINSON. *George Street from Grosvenor Street, showing James Underwood's house and the old jail.* □ *The low stone wall on the right surrounds the Male Orphan School. Next to it is the home of James Underwood, the shipbuilder, gin distiller and merchant, whose ship can be seen on the estuary of the Tank Stream. This flowed behind Underwood's house and here he built and repaired the ships that turned him from a penniless convict into one of Sydney's wealthiest merchants. When it was built by Underwood in 1804 this large stone house was considered much more luxurious than Government House. It stood on George Street for over one hundred years.*

The figure in a cocked hat wearing a brass kingplate round his neck is Bungaree, King of Sydney. On his left is the building of the Main Guard, with a sentry in a high stove-pipe shako on duty. The long white wall at the corner of George and Essex Streets encloses the grim and overcrowded Sydney jail, where hundreds of prisoners were hanged and flogged behind the arched gate. It is ironic that today the jail's spartan foundations lie buried beneath the luxurious Regent Hotel.

Louis de Sainson was the offical artist on board the French survey ship "Astrolabe" which visited Sydney in 1826. He was employed by the Navy to paint scenes of interest to be used as illustrations for Captain Dumont d'Urville's official account of the expedition which was published in 1830.

Bungaree, King of Sydney

The freelance travelling artist Augustus Earle probably hoped to recoup the costs of his world tour by publishing the drawings he made in many different countries on his return to London.

He left Sydney in October 1828, and for three months was the official artist on the *Beagle* but, due to recurring bouts of fever, he was forced to resign and was replaced by Conrad Martens. Earle then returned to London to find that the luxurious coffee-table book of his hand-coloured Australian lithographs entitled *Views in New South Wales and Van Diemen's Land* was selling quite successfully. His skilful drawings, combined with an interesting text, attracted the attention of Robert Burford, a leading entertainment impressario of Regency London. Burford was the proprietor of a large building in Leicester Square known as Burford's Panorama. In the era before cinema, this panorama provided the equivalent of a travel documentary.

Around its interior walls Burford commissioned life size paintings of a particular town. The audience sat in the centre, while a lecturer literally walked them through the streets and talked about the scenery, buildings and leading characters of the place. Burford felt that his viewers had seen enough of European cities and that a glimpse of the Antipodes by Augustus Earle would be an ideal novelty to fill his panorama every evening. It was something new and different for London since Earle was now becoming a well-known artist, specialising in scenes of exotic and unknown areas of the world.

The writer William Astley in his *Tales of the Early Days* described the scene as Earle's enormous panorama of Old Sydney Town, the Cove and The Rocks were unveiled for the first time to a packed audience. Perhaps Augustus Earle himself was the lecturer who described Sydney's buildings in detail. Astley did not say, but he certainly provided some of the information for the commentary. Astley's description is vivid and amusing. "The audience stirred in their seats, hankering to see the delights of Port Jackson, with the beautiful city of Sydney on its shores. They were sick of Italian cities, Mont Blanc and even Paris. But Sydney was something new and this was what they had paid their shillings to see. Terra Australis, or the great South Land of kangaroos and convicts, where the wicked went when the King was too merciful to hang them ... down on the other side of the world."

They leaned forward in their seats as Earle's great painting of the finest harbour in the world and its Georgian town were revealed, while the lecturer pointed out buildings like "the New Court House, a very respectable edifice facing Hyde Park, the Market House in George Street, built by Governor Macquarie, and Mrs Darling's School of Industry, for the reception of female children of convicts, who are by this school removed from the contagious example set them by vicious and dissolute parents ... and taught everything requisite to make them useful members of society." The jail was described as "insecure and scarcely adequate for the safe keeping of prisoners" They also saw the great George Street Military Barracks "a very substantial capacious and well-arranged series of buildings erected by Governor Macquarie in the most eligible part of town," the residence of Sir John Jamison, "a wealthy and extensive property" on today's Jamieson Street and "Cockle Bay" now Darling Harbour, "where Mr J. MacArthur, the father of Australian sheep husbandry is building his magnificent residence" and Fort Phillip, now used as a signal station.

To add more appeal to his scenes, Earle had carefully painted in several figures guaranteed to be of interest overseas. The three figures he chose were Governor Ralph Darling pictured out riding with his private secretary, a Captain Dumaresq, and Bungaree, King of Sydney and Broken Bay.

The audience loved Bungaree, seen waving his Admiral's cocked hat and wearing a cast-off uniform jacket, his cheery face wreathed in a huge smile. The commentary described how Bungaree, his wife and "a boat-load of his dingy retainers" were "generally the first visitors to board every ship on its arrival in Sydney Cove. Wearing his large brass plate proudly announcing his title of King of Sydney, His Majesty makes one stride from the gangway, lifts up his hat with the right hand a full foot from his head, and with all the grace and ease of a Court exquisite, he bids 'Massa' welcome in his own country." Clothed in an Admiral's blue jacket "ornamented with gold lace and massive gold epaulettes but without shirt or waistcoat, he welcomes the arrival of all strangers with much politeness and many bows, his bare and broad platter feet of dull cinder hue spreading out like a pair of sprawling toads. He only solicits the loan of a dump (a small coin) on pretence of treating his sick Queen to a cup of tea, but in reality with a view of treating himself to a porringer of Mr Cooper's best gin, to which His Majesty is most royally devoted."

The story of Bungaree, the King without a Kingdom was a great success at Burford's Panorama. He became a well-known figure overseas, mentioned by Governor Hunter, David Collins and Matthew Flinders in their historic accounts of the first settlement of Australia and painted by Earle, de Sainson, Carmichael and Rodius, as well as other artists from foreign scientific expeditions. Contemporary accounts describe Bungaree as "of medium build with a happy disposition and highly intelligent." He was the first Aboriginal to sail right around Australia, acting as interpreter for Matthew Flinders and Phillip Parker King. His name was spelt both as Bongaree or Bungaree. He proved to be loyal and courageous when Flinders was confronted by hostile Aboriginals at Bribie Island, Queensland, where the town of Bongaree was named after him.

Earle first painted King Bungaree's portrait in 1826. Despite his ragged trousers and bare feet Earle saw King Bungaree in a totally royal role. Nobility is suggested by the background of the imposing towers of Fort Macquarie and the *H.M.S. Warspite*, captained by Sir

James Brisbane, the first British warship ever to enter Sydney Harbour. According to Bungaree's epitaph in the *Sydney Gazette* "Sir James was particularly partial to Bungaree and presented him with a suit of his own Admiral's uniform, together with a sword, of which he was not a little vain."

Bungaree was equally proud of the uniform, which he wore day and night. He was also an accomplished mimic and could do perfect imitations of every Governor from Hunter to Brisbane. Unlike the majority of Aboriginals in Sydney at that period, he spoke good English, probably due to his long periods at sea. He was also noted for his sense of humour. His talents for amusing various governors and high officials coupled with his experience at sea and his natural dignity established him firmly as the leader of the township Aboriginals. The brass king-plate presented to him by Macquarie gave him no tribal authority, but a certain prestige with the white settlers. Macquarie instituted the custom of awarding king-plates in 1816. He held an annual feast at Parramatta when he talked with the appointed representatives from tribes as far away as Bathurst and Newcastle and as a symbol of authority gave each tribal leader a brass plate inscribed with his name. Bungaree had several wives named respectively as Boatman, Broomstick, Onion and Pincher, but it would appear that the sensual Queen Gooseberry or Matora was his favourite wife. She was described in 1820 by a Russian naval officer, P. Novosilsky, who visited Sydney with Bellingshausen's expedition, as "truly the personification of ugliness, but when I met her in the bush she always asked to be kissed". Presumably the gallant Russian officer obliged her because he then described how "weary to the point of exhaustion but rich in new impressions I returned to the ship very late in the evening!" Bellingshausen himself described his meeting with Queen Matora or Cora Gooseberry and Bungaree when, "indicating his companions as he came on board Bungaree said 'These are my people.' Then, pointing at the whole North Shore he said 'This is my shore!' They asked for tobacco and old clothes ... and left the ship half-drunk. Matora or Gooseberry called herself Queen, but behaved with more sexual abandon than all the other guests."

*Plate 32   AUGUSTUS EARLE. **King Bungaree, c.1826**. Oil on canvas. Rex Nan Kivell Collection, National Library of Australia.*

Bungaree, the King Without
a Kingdom

Several years after the portrait, Augustus Earle made a lithographed drawing of Bungaree for inclusion in his book. The differences between the two pictures sum up the whole tragic story of the decline of the Aboriginals. Bungaree, with the exception of a few wrinkles looks just the same, but Earle has subtly told the whole story of Bungaree's downfall by his subtle change of background. Instead of the nobility of Fort Macquarie, the scene is now set at The Rocks and the two bottles of grog in the foreground tell their own story. Beside Bungaree is Matora or Cora Gooseberry, Queen of Sydney to South Head, whose own breastplate and rum mug are today preserved in the Mitchell Library.

In 1815 Macquarie gave Bungree and his group some land to farm at South Head, complete with the necessary tools and stock and a convict to instruct them in planting crops. This proved a failure, but later Governor Sir Thomas Brisbane gave them a fishing boat and a net, which proved considerably more suited to their way of life. Bungaree's obituary in the *Sydney Gazette* occupied a full page and stated that when he was very ill, Alexander MacLeay arranged for Bungaree to be admitted to the Rum Hospital "where he received every attention and remained some weeks but becoming impatient to return to his people he was permitted to depart." After a lingering sickness he died at Garden Island and was buried at Rose Bay.

*Plate 33   AUGUSTUS EARLE. **King Bungaree, a Native Chief of New South Wales.** Hand coloured lithograph, published London 1830. National Library of Australia.*

KING BUNGAREE.

CHIEF, OF THE BROKEN-BAY TRIBE, N.S.WALES

DIED. 1832.

*Plate 34 CHARLES RODIUS. **King Bungaree.** Lithograph published 1834, after Bungaree's death. Photograph courtesy Timothy and Ann McCormick*

The final portrait of The King without a Kingdom was made not by the merry traveller, Augustus Earle but by a tragic and perceptive French convict artist named Charles Rodius who, while on a visit to London, was transported for stealing a suitcase.

Rodius arrived in Sydney in 1829 and was immediately assigned to teach colonial government and military officials the art of topographical drawing. He was also engaged by the colonial architect to produce plans of every building in Australia at that time. In 1831 he began issuing the first of his remarkable series of lithographed portraits of the Aboriginal "Kings" and their "Queens". These portraits aroused a great deal of interest in Sydney and overseas and the *Sydney Monitor* commented that Rodius used "the lithographic press with great skill. He has executed front and profile likenesses of Bungaree in a most superior style."

Rodius' compassionate view of Bungaree was undoubtedly his masterpiece in this series. Bungaree's whole face has changed since he was drawn by Earle. His features are etched with poverty and malnutrition and coarsened by alcohol. Around his neck is still proudly worn the second of his king-plates over cast-off naval clothing from yet another begging foray to an incoming ship. This type of adornment dated from the time of the Pharoahs. Similar plates were also presented to North American Indian chiefs and were generally made of silver. These solid brass cast plates given by the Governors are extremely rare today, whereas the later thin hammered plates given to the Aboriginals by the squatters are still relatively common, although unique to Australia. His king-plate represents a tragic and futile attempt to bridge two totally different cultures and their opposing values. The story of Bungaree is the story of The King who became famous but was defeated by an alien way of life in his own Kingdom of Sydney.

George Street in 1798

Plate 35   THOMAS WATLING. **Old Barracks in George Street.** *Mitchell Library.*

This view of the Old Barracks in George Street was made by convict artist, Thomas Watling. After the departure of Surgeon John White in 1794, Watling was re-assigned as a general servant to Judge-Advocate David Collins and to provide drawings for Collins' *Account of the English Colony in New South Wales* which was published in 1798. The original drawing is believed to be in the Mitchell Library.

Watling, an intelligent and sensitive young man, was unhappy and angry at his harsh treatment in Sydney where he described himself as forced "to toil like a slave ... in poverty, sickness and sorrow." It is hardly surprising that his view of George Street and its first Barracks made it look so bleak and forbidding. The squalid mud and wattle huts or slab cottages of the convicts, with their dirt floors and unglazed windows gave poor shelter against sun or rain, since the concept of the verandah had not yet been imported from India. But few other cities retain a record of such early views.

In Watling's time this part of George Street leading towards the Tank Stream was known as Spring Row, and this was the only street in the whole of Australia. Behind it lay clusters of unnumbered and unsanitary convict cottages known as "Rows".

On the extreme right of Watling's engraved drawing, soldiers are marching into the old wooden barracks, which were hastily built out of timber in 1788-9. Their unseasoned timbers gradually rotted and Macquarie replaced them with the much larger brick barracks, which were vacated in 1848. The whole fifteen-acre area was surveyed, divided into blocks and sold to commercial concerns between 1850 and 1853.

It seems scarcely possible that only some ninety years separate the two widely differing views of George Street by Watling and Tischbauer. Seen together for the first time, these two paintings sum up more graphically than any commentary the remarkable development of Australia's first street.

Tischbauer was a Frenchman from Alsace who had been actively involved in the Paris Communes of 1871 and, like Lucien Henry, was sent to New Caledonia as a punishment. He had trained as a scene painter and designer and worked at the Paris Opera. Finding little opportunity for his sophisticated sets in Sydney, he stayed only a few years and then went on to New York where he became a successful stage designer. Tischbauer's George Street is the epitome of Victorian

George Street in 1883

Plate 36   *ALFRED J. TISCHBAUER.* **George Street in 1883.** *Oil, Dixson Galleries.*

respectability. Prosperous businessmen in top hats stroll along its pavements accompanied by elegant ladies with parasols, possibly on their way to shop at Thompson & Giles, who advertised themselves as "The Busy Drapers and Haberdashers" and were situated beside the lane that was eventually widened to form Martin Place. The famous G.P.O. clock had just been moved to overhang George Street, since pedestrians complained they were unable to see the time when it was originally set into the facade of the G.P.O. building. In the right-hand foreground two rival banks, the Commercial and the New South Wales shared a handsome building with richly decorated windows.

In 1882 the Gibbs Shallard *Guide to Sydney* describing itself as "a manual replete with information for strangers" commented on the remarkable transformation of this part of George Street in less than a century, describing how "time has worked wonders and the barrack walls, the barren parade ground and uncomfortable quarters of officers and men have now given way to princely edifices, whose total money value must be reckoned in hundreds of thousands ... Here stands the Bank of New South Wales, affording the thrifty a safe means of investing their hoards ... while the Commercial Bank, a flourishing institution, occupies the front corner."

The Building of the Town Hall

In 1842 John Rae had just applied for the job of Town Clerk. Perhaps this is the reason that he made this drawing of the Old Burial Ground. The first Council did not possess a Town Hall or a suitable site for one, and its first two meetings were held in the old Markets Buildings on George Street. For another year the Council tried meeting in various places but, in April, 1843, they requested the Governor to grant them the site of the Old Burial Ground in George Street. However the General Cemetery Bill failed to be passed by the Legislative Council, whose permission was needed to deconsecrate the burial ground and the measure was dropped. Rae was finally awarded the position of Town Clerk in July of that year but, without a Town Hall to work from, it proved a difficult appointment. For many years he was forced to put up with cramped and temporary office accommodation, constant moves and an inadequate staff.

The Council requested various other sites without success, before approaching the Government a second time for permission to use the Old Burial Ground. This time, some 26 years later, the Council's request was granted. Finally a new Town Hall was to be built on the site. The legend still persists around Sydney that there are numerous convict skeletons under the first Town Hall. The coffins were carted off and re-buried in the Devonshire Street Cemetery. This was not their final resting place and they had to be moved again to the Botany Cemetery when the Central Railway Station was built, so it was scarcely eternal repose for the convict dead.

Once they had been granted a site for the erection of their new Town Hall, the Council held competitions for the design of the building. Mr J. Wilson won both first and second prizes. It was subsequently found, much to everyone's embarrassment, that he had designed two prize-winning buildings which were quite beyond the technical competence of any nineteenth-century builder to construct. Edward Bell, the City Surveyor, was instructed to prepare simplified plans, based on one of Wilson's designs, but the final supervision and alterations were left to Alfred Bond who designed the Town Hall vestibule. Prince Alfred, Duke of Edinburgh, son of Queen Victoria, laid the foundation stone on 4th April, 1868. During his Sydney visit he was the victim of an anarchist's assassination attempt at the Clontarf Pic-nic Races but it was unsuccessful. He recovered and sailed away leaving the foundation stone as his contribution. This was the first visit by a member of the Royal Family and it was felt that Sydney's Town Hall had been duly assured of future prestige by his presence. A larger Centennial or Main Hall was planned for completion in the Centenary year of 1888.

The Town Hall itself is an amazing mixture of architectural styles, containing a French mansarded roof like a chateau, an Italian campanile or bell-tower, Greek classical pediments and a double-stair, all incongruously flanked by Moorish and Romanesque arches.

Perhaps its conflicting architectural messages proved too confusing for many artists, but today there are few paintings of the Town Hall in all its glory. Its clock Tower, which has always been known as one of Sydney's outstanding landmarks, described by local wits as the "Bondi Renaissance style" was completed in 1881. Delays followed in obtaining the mechanism of the clock, which was not installed until three years later, and the chimes were added in 1885.

The Town Hall was officially opened in 1880 and Commissioners from the International Exhibition held at the Garden Palace were officially entertained in the new building. An enormous crystal chandelier was installed in the ceiling and large bronze tablets were designed to record the names of important interstate and overseas visitors. The unfortunate Prince Alfred, Duke of Edinburgh, so nearly murdered at Clontarf, had his picture hung on the northern stairway, perhaps as a warning to future members of the Royal Family against the dangers of laying foundation stones in Australia.

The best known engraving of the Town Hall was made to celebrate Australia's first centenary. A mammoth three-volume publication entitled *The Picturesque Atlas of Australasia* was planned and Frederick Schell, the Art Editor of a similar Canadian publication was invited to Sydney to commission suitable artists and select the views for the book. Some of Australia's finest artists, such as Julian Ashton and Arthur Fullwood, were commissioned to travel around Australia, painting the most beautiful as well as the most historically interesting views.

Schell also executed this view of the newly-built Town Hall with Edmund Blacket's Cathedral of St. Andrews in the background, which had just been finished. Schell's view of the Town Hall was designed to show Sydney at its most prosperous. Well-dressed people stroll along the kerbed pavements, horse omnibuses and coaches suggest the increasing wealth of the colony.

The Town Hall with its international pot-pourri of architectural styles was seen as a symbol of the power and stability of both Sydney and Australia. Now it is admired for its sheer opulence and optimism in the future of a great city, even though it is still curiously enough named the "Town" rather than "City" Hall.

Plate 37 JOHN RAE. **The site of the Town Hall.** *George Street looking north towards Druitt Street in 1842. Signed and dated watercolour. Dixson Galleries.* □ *John Rae, the future Town Clerk, drew the old Convict Burial Ground, surrounded by a high wall, which was to become the site of the Town Hall. He also showed the round dome of the Old Police Office, at one time used by the Customs Department, the first market buildings. To the extreme left behind the Old Burial Ground are the pointed spires of the first Jewish Synagogue in Australia. This end of George Street still has a distinctly rustic air. Bullock carts drag in enormous trunks of timber, possibly to be used in the building of St. Andrew's Cathedral.*

Plate 38 FREDERICK SCHELL. **The Town Hall and St. Andrew's Cathedral.** *Hand-coloured wood engraving c.1887. □ Schell's picture shows a prosperous-looking population in front of their new Town Hall. The original Town Hall is now the vestibule. The great auditorium was built later and named the Centennial Hall to mark the hundredth anniversary of Australia. This engraving was designed for inclusion in "The Picturesque Atlas of Australasia." These were three large illustrated volumes designed to record Australia's progress over one hundred years.*

George Street and the Gold Rush

CORNER OF GEORGE AND MARKET STREETS, WEST SYDNEY.

Plate 39 LASSETTER'S **The Ironmongers, 421 George Street.** *Unsigned hand-tinted lithograph. Artist unknown c.1865-1870. Photograph courtesy Joseph Lebovic Gallery, Paddington.* □ *In 1864 Frederick Lassetter purchased premises at 421 George Street with the money that he had made selling picks, shovels, cradles, and tin dishes to the miners who flocked to the goldfields. The gold rush was a bonanza for George Street's stores and many of their owners acquired wealth beyond their wildest dreams. Often there was more profit in selling shovels and cradles than in actually going off to the goldfields.*

From these premises Lassetter gradually purchased the surrounding shops until, by 1888, Lassetter's Cheapside employed over a thousand people both selling and manufacturing and had a fleet of 40 horse-drawn delivery-vans, similar to the one which stands outside the store in the picture. Lassetter supplied hardware to squatters and tradesmen all round Australia by mail order.

The First Post Office in Australia

Captain Owen Stanley of the *H.M.S. Rattlesnake* and convict artist John Carmichael both painted the old market place, the main commerical centre of old Sydney. Today this part of George Street south of Globe Street lies under the overpass of the Cahill Expressway. Carmichael's engraving shows the bullock drays that were used to unload the ships from the Queen's Wharf that lay behind George Street. In 1847, eighteen years later, the area was still an official waiting place for drays, but the bullocks have been replaced by horses. Captain Stanley shows one of the carts belonging to the famous Sydney water carriers. They delivered water to Sydney's householders for twopence per bucket from the clear waters of the Lachlan and Blackwattle Swamps, since the Tank Stream was then too polluted to provide drinking water.

Carmichael clearly shows the passage that led down to the wharf and the masts of the sailing ships that were moored alongside. To the right of the lane was one of Sydney's leading ships' chandlers, Messrs Kemp and Dobson. On the right of Kemp and Dobson, with its distinctive verandah, was the house of Isaac Nichols, a former convict, whose capacity for hard work had already earned him the important position of Assistant Naval Officer, helping collect customs and harbour dues. However there were no postmen for the delivery of letters and parcels which arrived on board these ships.

For 26 years after the first settlement of New South Wales there were also no regular post offices. Official communications and despatches were carried by constables, who occasionally carried letters for the settlers. On 25th April 1809 Lieutenant Governor William Paterson made the historic proclamation which established the first Post Office in Australia.

"Complaints have been made that numerous frauds have been committed by individuals impersonating others, by which they have obtained possession of letters and valuable parcels, to the great injury of those for whom they were intended. In order to prevent such frauds the Lieutenant-Governor has to establish an office, at which all parcels and letters are to be deposited, under the direction of Mr Isaac Nichols, the Assistant to the Naval Officer, who has entered into a security for the faithful discharge of the trust reposed in him."

It was felt that a man of strong and powerful character and maritime experience was needed for the job of Postmaster as well as ownership of premises in a central location for the collection of mail since the first postal service had no delivery boys and all mail had to be collected and paid for at Nichols' house. Nichols was authorised to "board all vessels arriving and require in the King's name that all letters and parcels delivered to the Colony be handed over to him." Every letter carried a collection charge of one shilling in addition to a further high transport fee and so to save money they were often written both horizontally and vertically over the paper and the recipient often spent many hours deciphering the longed-for letter.

In 1810 Macquarie, pleased with the efficient way in which Nichols ran this post office from his George Street general store, prolonged his appointment for a further term and gave him the additional responsibility of Superintendent of Convicts. Nichols, who was married to the daughter of Esther Julian of Annandale, became a wealthy man and died in 1819. His job as postmaster was taken over by wharf owner George Panton, whose family lived in the house for many years. After Panton's death the postmaster's job was given to a Mr James Raymond, who ran the post office from Bent Street. By 1838 the postal system had grown into a powerful network and there were daily deliveries of letters around Sydney instead of the old system of collection from the post office.

Captain Owen Stanley was aged 36 when he made this watercolur. He kept sketchbooks of drawings made on his voyages of exploration to show his family in England on his return and helped establish the northern colony at Port Essington, transporting stores and men on board his ship the *Britomart*.

In 1846 he received command of the survey ship *H.M.S. Rattlesnake* and arrived in Sydney accompanied by the naturalist, T. H. Huxley. He stayed there for several months refitting and reprovisioning the ship and met Oswald Brierly at Bloxsome's home "The Rangers" in Mosman. The two men became friends and Brierly was invited to accompany the *Britomart* on her voyage northwards. Stanley charted considerable sections of the north-east Australian coastline and south-east New Guinea. He died on 15th March, 1850 in Sydney and, as a mark of respect to the importance of his Australian survey work, all the shops along George Street were closed on the day of his funeral. He was given a funeral cortege of boats across the harbour and 250 men of the 11th Regiment followed his coffin to its burial at St. Thomas Church at St. Leonard's. This unique view shows George Street in its most important years as Sydney's High Street.

Plate 40

Plate 41 CAPTAIN OWEN STANLEY. **George Street in 1847 showing the First Post Office and the Main Guard.** *Watercolour from the artist's sketchbook. Mitchell Library.* □ *A similar view made thirteen years later by S. T. Gill shows how the street has been levelled for the passage of carriages in front of today's Regent Hotel.*

(left) JOHN CARMICHAEL. **George Street From the Wharf** *(detail) Copper engraving, 1829.*
□ *The house on the left of Captain Owen Stanley's watercolour was Australia's first post office run from a store owned by Isaac Nichols, a former convict. After his death the business was taken over by a wharf owner, George Panton, whose name is still painted on the wall. Adjacent to Isaac Nichols', house with an identical verandah, is the house of Mary Reiby, today a legend around The Rocks.*
   An excellent business woman and former convict, she was transported as a young girl for a joy-ride on a stolen pony. After her husband's death she ran a bakery, a shipping business and a general store with great efficiency.

David Jones Opens in George Street

In fact George Street looks more like elegant Bond Street than Oxford Street. Everyone looks prosperous and well dressed and smart canvas awnings stretch across the street to shield shoppers from the sun.

Facing David Jones was the Post Office, once the site of the Old Police Station, with its handsome stone portico which was added on about 1848, supported by an imposing set of columns. But this building soon became inadequate for the postal service and was demolished. Two of the old columns have been preserved under the Harbour Bridge by the site of Luna Park, one is now off Bradley's Head and two went to Vaucluse House as part of the entrance gates.

Large temporary weatherboard premises for the Post Office were provided at Wynyard Square, while the new G.P.O. was being built. They stretched from Wynyard Street to Margaret Street bounded by York Street on the west and Carrington Street on the east. The temporary Wynyard Square Post Office remained in use until the magnificent new G.P.O. in George Street was opened to the public on 21st September, 1874.

From its modest start in 1838, the David Jones store continued to prosper. David Jones purchased a further acre of land beside the store so that bullock drivers, horsemen and teamsters could tether their carts and carriages while they shopped, showing great foresight in providing possibly the first off-street parking of Sydney's Victorian era. David Jones was also the first to introduce "mail order shopping" whereby orders were received through the Cobb and Co. depot in Pitt Street and despatched anywhere in Australia by Cobb and Co. coaches. He used his English contacts and imported "large quantities of goods unsurpassed by any other house in the Colony" and George Street and David Jones appeared to thrive together. But by 1842 Australia was involved in a panic-ridden wave of depression.

Many banks failed, as well as numerous commercial establishments and stores on George Street. The astute David Jones cut down his overheads, sat tight and weathered the storm which finished many of his competitors.

During the next decade, the gold rush had an enormous effect on the prosperity of George Street. Terry's view reflects this prosperity in the people and carriages that throng the street, bringing wealth to the street's stores. By 1857 David Jones felt that it was safe to retire from the business, and sold out to Messrs. Thompson and Simmonds. The new firm gradually went down in reputation. Five years later David Jones was forced to sell off his beautiful home and come back and rescue the business, which was nearly bankrupt under its trading name of Thompson and Simmonds. But in 1860 the name David Jones once more appeared in George Street and, on the day of the grand opening, crowds gathered to cheer the elderly Welsh merchant, who had done so much for Australian commercial standards.

Although David Jones was always known for his honest trading, there were many less scrupulous shops in George Street. In convict days, George Street's jewellers had an unsavoury reputation. Thieves and fences sent their stolen jewellery out from London by sea to their convict associates, who sold it to Sydney's jewellers or, in some cases, set up in business themselves once they had obtained their convict pardon. An Army officer's wife was walking along George Street, where she saw her own jewellery, stolen from her the previous year in London, facing her on display in a shop window. When some distinguishing marks on the pieces were pointed out to him, the jeweller hastily returned the goods. It was reckoned that a high percentage of Britain's stolen jewellery and silver eventually wound up for sale on George Street.

In 1846 Lt. Colonel Mundy described how "I passed my first Australian evening rambling slowly up George Street, the main artery of the city and down Pitt Street, the Broadway and the Oxford Street of the Antipodes." Perhaps he passed by David Jones small emporium on George Street at the corner of Barrack Lane. Here in 1838 this middle-aged Welsh merchant, who had been a grocer's apprentice at fourteen, opened his second shop in Sydney. The first David Jones store was on Pitt Street, but George Street at that period was considered an infinitely more prestigious address. David Jones came to the George Street site after having been in partnership with Charles Appleton. However on 24th May 1838 Jones advertised that "having dissolved his partnership with Mr Appleton, he has removed his business to these large and commodious premises opposite the General Post Office in George Street, where he will receive his usual consignments of goods from England. He avails himself of this opportunity to return his most grateful thanks for the support he has received and begs to solicit a continuance of public patronage."

The first shop on the left shows David Jones' emporium, with its plain cast-iron balcony on the first floor and tall oval windows. A salesman stands outside the door to welcome the occupants of the smart carriage which has just arrived in Barrack Lane and to guide them into the store.

Plate 42 FREDERICK CHARLES TERRY. **George Street looking north towards the junction of today's Martin Place.** *Wood engraving from the 1850s. Mitchell Library.* □ *The building on the extreme left with the iron balcony is David Jones' first George Street store, possibly with David Jones himself or one of his assistants waiting to greet prospective customers, who have arrived by coach at Barrack Lane. Further along are the Commercial and New South Wales banks, separated by two shops.*

In those days these banks were bitter rivals, but now this feud has been buried in recent amalgamation. The facade of the original Commercial Bank building was taken down and re-erected within the grounds of the University of Sydney. On the right is the Post Office with its six Doric classical columns, one of which is now at Bradley's Head, one near Luna Park and two used as gateposts for Vaucluse House. Although the footway is paved and kerbed, the road still appears dusty and unmade. Terry shows a wonderful mixture of Sydney's inhabitants. A wealthy squatter and his wife ride down the centre of the street, hansom cabs are offered for hire and the whole area reflects the prosperity of Australia in the gold-rush period. In fact this corner of George Street was often known as "The Golden Corner."

The Power and Prestige
of the Post Office

One of the most important elements of their new life for many recent migrants to Australia was news from home. Due to the tyranny of distance, many realised that they would never see their relatives again and, in the era before the telephone, the receipt of mail from Britain was of enormous emotional significance.

Before rapid telecommunications became widely established, the Post Office wielded enormous power and prestige, and the magnificent Sydney building of the General Post Office reflected this power.

The building was designed by the colonial architect, James Barnet and construction work on the building started in 1874. It was built in several stages, and the first section of the Post Office extended from George Street through to the western side of the present Martin Place entrance.

The whole building was rendered even more imposing by a severe and regal statue of Queen Victoria, somewhat incongruously flanked by an assembly of semi-naked ancient Greek goddesses, over the main entrance. The building and its grounds covered an enormous area and, as late as the end of the 1870s, the horses that carried the postmen and post-office messenger boys were quartered in the grounds of the George Street G.P.O.

The post-office messenger boys shown in this wood engraving rode around the streets of Sydney collecting the mail from the beautiful cast-iron letter-boxes ornamented with decorations of engraved acanthus leaves. Today there is still one of these post-boxes left standing in Argyle Place. The mail was delivered to householders by postmen in forage caps or white pith helmets, scarlet jackets, brass buttoned jackets with cross-belts and serge trousers with a stripe down each side. They carried Her Majesty's mail in huge leather satchels, and appeared to be about to announce the relief of Mafeking or the personal commands of Queen Victoria, rather than just deliver a simple letter from relatives in Britain. But they also contributed to making the receipt of the longed-for overseas mail into an event.

The same feeling of prestige was reflected in the handsome and vast halls and staircases of the G.P.O. Building with "its lofty and majestic tower, which is such a conspicuous landmark from all parts of the city. Its foundations descend thirty feet in the rock below the pavement line, with very strong arches over the sewer of the Tank Stream, as its flow could not be interfered with in any way." This description was published in the *Sydney Morning Herald* in 1887.

The arcades of the Post Office were one of Sydney's more important meeting places. Under these handsome granite columns was an ornately-carved notice board made out of cedar with gold lettering. It measured some 10 feet long and gave all the latest information concerning shipping arrivals, showing when mail would be in from different towns in Australia and overseas. At this period it was actually quicker to send a letter to many isolated towns in Australia by sea than by the bad roads.

W.C. Smedley's original drawing was made for *The Picturesque Atlas of Australasia* to celebrate Australia's first centenary. It shows the arcade with the businessmen, soldiers and messenger-boys who flocked to George Street's Palace of the Postage Stamp to collect their letters or to promenade there, both to see and be seen.

Plate 43
Collecting the mail in Sydney. *Wood engraving by an unknown artist c.1886.*

Plate 44 W. C. SMEDLEY. **The Arcade of the General Post Office.** *Wood engraving c.1886. From "The Picturesque Atlas of Australasia."*

The Old George Street Markets

In 1810 Macquarie found that market stalls crowded high with vegetables, poultry and dried foodstuffs made access to the King's Wharf from George Street North difficult. He issued orders that "the present Market-Place being very badly and inconveniently situated, it is His Excellency's intention to remove the Market to a more commodious and central situation for the Inhabitants of the Town. The Place thus intended for the new Market is the open ground (part of which was lately used by Mr Blaxland as a Stockyard) bounded by George Street on the East, York Street on the West, Market Street on the North and the Burial Ground on the South, henceforth to be called "Market Square." For the convenience of the Inhabitants and particularly for those bringing Corn or other Grain and Merchandise in Boats from the Hawkesbury to the Market, it is intended to erect a Wharf at Cockle Bay continuous to the new Market Place."

The road from the wharf to the markets became known as Market Street. The dome building of the Market House, originally designed by Francis Greenway, appears in John Rae's view entitled *George Street looking North* on Page 51.

In 1827 Surgeon Peter Cunningham described the "commodious Market House with ... a row of wooden sheds where the traders trick out their showy wares while numerous stands are crowded with the various products of English or colonial manufacture. The whole is placed under the charge of an officer named Clerk of the Market, and good order is preserved throughout by the beneficial regulations in force. It is held on Thursdays, and attended by individuals from a distance of forty miles or more, with the produce of their agricultural industry. During the preceding day, as you journey toward the interior, you will encounter file after file of carts, loaded with wheat, maize, potatoes, peas, carrots, turnips, cabbages, fruit, pigs, calves, poultry, and indeed all sorts of commodities for culinary use, pouring along the road toward Sydney."

In 1828 the Market House became the headquarters of the police and Druitt Street was laid out, in order to divide the new Police Station from the old Burial Ground. By 1831 new Market Buildings were under construction from drawings made by Ambrose Allen, the Government Architect.

Each building was 200 feet long and 30 feet wide divided into stalls for the sale of meat, poultry and dairy produce, and for fruit and vegetables. On the George Street side were all types of household goods at wholesale prices. The George Street Market was visited by strangers and townsfolk alike, especially on a Saturday evening and "few, if any, who visited Sydney thought of leaving without paying them a visit. From the elegance of the building it appeared as an amphitheatre rather than a public market."

This picture was painted by William Brookes Spong, a talented artist who had worked as a scenic designer at the great Theatre Royal, Drury Lane in London. He painted some of the scenery for the first production of Gilbert and Sullivan's *Trial by Jury* and exhibited at the Royal Academy in London and the Royal Institute of Painters in Watercolours. He arrived in Sydney in 1887 as scene designer for the Brough and Boucicault Company and received the first Government grant to the arts ever made in Australia. In order to preserve some pictorial records of the rapidly vanishing colonial Sydney, Julian Ashton persuaded the current Minister for Works, The Hon E. O'Sullivan to grant a sum of money to commission a series of fifteen pictures by artists such as William Brookes Spong, Julian Ashton himself and and H. Stuart-Wilson.

After some time W. B. Spong went into theatrical management in Sydney, starring his own daughter in a series of productions. He also exhibited with the Royal Art Society of Sydney and the Victorian Artists' Exhibition. He eventually returned to London where he died at the age of 78 but left behind in Sydney this superbly painted view of the old Market Buildings which were eventually replaced in 1893 by the Queen Victoria Building. This massive Victorian monument was regarded by many as a sandstone extravaganza and Sydney's white elephant. Soon after it opened one wit described it as "a monument to civic energy and a chronic economic headache." The building fell quickly on hard times even though its architecture was striking, with delicate balustrades, a large copper dome and a glass roof which flooded the interior with natural light. The Council gutted the interior and installed office accommodation and the City Library, while parts of the building lay derelict for nearly 20 years. A Malaysian company, Ipoh Garden Berhad, won an international competition calling for tenders to fund the building's restoration. The building opened with due ceremony in November 1986, complete with statue of Queen Victoria and a series of pictures of her life from cradle to grave.

Plate 45   WILLIAM SPONG. **Old George Street Markets.** *Watercolour. Dixson Galleries, Sydney.*

Plate 46 *JOHN RAE.* **George and Bathurst Streets in 1842 looking south towards Brickfield Hill.** *Signed and dated watercolour. Dixson Galleries.*

Visitors to Sydney in the 1840s were often surprised at the high price of books that all had to be imported from England, since few were printed in Sydney at this period. They were also amazed to find that Sydney's Cathedral was nothing but a large weatherboard building, with none of the mediaeval splendour that English and European immigrants had come to expect from a cathedral. This was due to a shortage of funds and although Macquarie had planned a great cathedral for Sydney his plans had been drastically curtailed, and the cathedral was not completed for many years. The shortage and high cost of books was a problem for many Sydney residents both for pleasure and educational purposes, and also for designs for anyone building a home who wanted to copy the latest English buildings.

One of the most interesting men in the book trade was Jerry Moore, who later became world-famous as a result of his publication of *Old Moore's Almanac.*

The enterprising Moore owned one of Australia's first bookshops on the future site of the cathedral, which was then under construction. The building just behind Moore's Bookstall was occupied by Francis Croker, verger of the temporary rough weatherboard cathedral which had been opened in 1842. Four years later, Edmund Blacket took over supervision of the permanent stone building, which he designed in

traditional English mediaeval style, with a tower copied from Magdalen College, Oxford. Building work continued in fits and starts, as and when funds permitted, and St Andrew's was eventually consecrated and opened in 1868.

The noise and dirt from the cathedral's construction would have made it difficult for Jerry Moore to run his outdoor bookstall with its home-made bookcases, which he had moved from various locations around Sydney. His success was due to his own unique method of book purchase. When an immigrant ship arrived from England, Jerry would row out to sea and board it. The emigrants, worried about their finances in a new country, were only too happy to accept a ludicrously low price for the books which they had read and re-read many times on the long voyage. By the time they had landed and seen the high price of books on sale elsewhere in Sydney it was too late, and Moore had sold their books to his regular customers. The other attraction of his stall was a bucket of cold beer which he kept behind these bookstalls with a few mugs for the "regulars." Presumably the attraction of free beer compensated for the gloomy conditions of the Old Burial Ground, where pigs and goats wandered unchecked among the old tombstones of the First Fleeters, before the cathedral and Town Hall were built.

Plate 47   ALEXANDER HUEY. **The Pilot's House, Watson's Bay, 1810.** *Pen and wash drawing. Public Record Office of Northern Ireland. □ According to an old diary recently discovered in the Public Record Office of Belfast, Alexander Huey was a young lieutenant in the 73rd Regiment of Foot who accompanied the newly appointed Governor of New South Wales, Lachlan Macquarie, and his wife on their journey to Sydney at the end of 1809. Lieutenant Huey described how they "dropped anchor about 12 yards from the shore on December 30th. The band played and a party of about sixteen natives assembled round a fire on shore and danced, singing songs and beating time on a shield. The next day the Governor landed."*

On Monday, 1st January, the 73rd Regiment landed at Government Wharf at 10 a.m. and marched up to the Barracks where, after standing at attention for nearly half an hour, the Governor and his lady came into the Square accompanied by Sydney's leading figures and their wives. The young Alexander recounted how Macquarie made a "short but able speech to the troops and inhabitants of Sydney. The 73rd Regiment wheeled into line and marched out to Grose Farm Camp [now the site of Sydney University] about 3 miles from Sydney where we arrived at 2 o'clock." They found all the tents pitched but nothing to eat but potatoes. "Our breakfast consisted of potatoes and water. However in the course of a week we could procure bread and coffee or tea. Bread was very dear, being one shilling for a twopenny loaf. Two large snakes were killed in the camp and the whole regiment was busily employed burning the stumps of trees which prevented us drilling."

For the next three months Alexander Huey, who was encouraged to take up painting by John Lewin, explored Sydney town and its surrounding bays, making sketches of the land and the Aboriginals to take home. He first made pencil drawings of landscapes, often from a boat, and then made a finished watercolour on dry land. His portraits show far more talent than his landscapes and he wrote down various words in Aboriginal dialect under them. His little view of Watson's Bay shows an idyllic paradise of sand and sea with the Signal Station mast on the far right.

Lieutenant Huey was chosen to take Governor Macquarie's first despatches back to the British Government, after which he settled down amongst his family as a member of Ireland's landed gentry.

St. Mark's, Darling Point

Edmund Blacket's exquisite church with its lancet windows, once described as "a little sugar-castle church on a cake" provides one of the most charming and historic wedding venues in Australia. Its delicate spire now dominates the skyline of Darling Point and its parish includes Bellevue Hill and Double Bay. The first recorded marriage there took place on April 22nd, 1853, when the foundation stone had only been laid for five years, on land kindly donated by the tycoon, T. S. Mort. Prior to the building of St. Mark's there had been no church east of St. James.

The church drawn by Gill and Hardwick was smaller than the one today, since it lacked a vestry. This was due to shortage of labour during its construction, as any man in Sydney capable of wielding a spade was off to the goldfields rather than building churches. But by 1864 the church was completed, with the exception of its slender spire which was not added until the 1870s. Although Hardwick's drawing dated 1853 shows a church steeple, this was drawn in by the artist, who made his drawing to send to relatives overseas. Probably to make it look more impressive he added in the spire as projected, choosing one of the fourteen designs Blacket submitted to the parish for approval. He noted "spire unfinished but will be octagonal."

Both Hardwick and Gill showed the church when Darling Point was a friendly village. After morning service T. S. Mort kept open house at his neighbouring baronial mansion, Greenoaks. Churchgoers were served with light refreshments and could view his collection of old master paintings, comtemporary watercolours, suits of armour and French furniture which he had acquired from Alton Towers, the home of the Earl of Salisbury. J. Hardwick's watercolour dated 1853 is from the Mitchell Library and S. T. Gill's from the Dixson Library, signed and dated 1857.

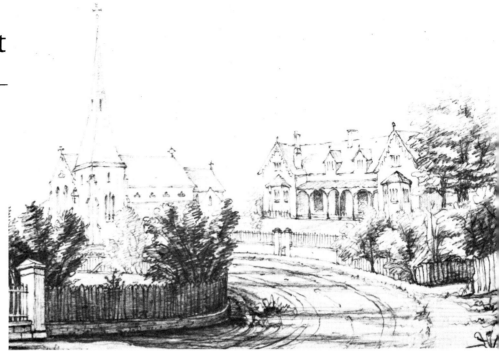

Plate 48   JOHN HARDWICK. **St Mark's Darling Point.** *Watercolour, 1853. Mitchell Library.*

Plate 49   S. T. GILL. **St Mark's Darling Point.** *Watercolour, 1857 Dixson Library.*

St James', King Street

Greenway originally designed St. James', King Street, as Sydney's Court House while a church was to be built on the site of today's Town Hall. Commissioner Bigge found this superb Colonial Georgian building "an indulgence" for the trials of convicts and ordered Greenway to convert it into a church. Next to it Greenway was instructed to build the severely plain Court House which appeared in Robert Russell's lithograph. This lithographed drawing, printed by J. G. Austin in 1836 showed a bleak St. James' in a rough convict settlement where even the copper sheathing on the church spire had to be marked with the broad arrow to prevent pilfering by the inhabitants. These same convicts were forced by Macquarie to attend church on Sundays wearing "clean white trowsers," segregated from the fashionable congregation in a secluded gallery with its own special entrance.

When Gill drew the church in 1856, a wedding at St. James' was essential for anyone aspiring to polite society. Its Register of Christenings and Marriages still reads like a Debrett's Peerage of early Australia. At night, however, St. James' presented a totally different picture. The Illustrated Sydney News for October 29, 1853 described how anyone returning home alone after dark waited outside the church until a group had assembled so they could cross Hyde park together, as the park had an evil reputation for night robberies and muggings. The newspaper concluded, "We find it extraordinary that the inhabitants of civilised Sydney in the 1850s should be placed in the circumstances of an eastern desert caravan."

Plate 50   J. G. AUSTIN. **St James', King Street.** *Lithograph, 1836.*

Plate 51   S. T. GILL. **St James', King Street.** *Drawing, 1856.*

The Saga of the Governors' Residences

Governor Phillip wisely brought his own temporary residence with him. It was a canvas and timber hut which leaked badly in Sydney's storms and he lived in it for eleven months, while the first Government House was built. In July 1789 Phillip wrote to Lord Stanley that "the house intended for myself was to consist of only three rooms but having a good foundation has been enlarged to six rooms." Work was slow. Sydney had only three trained carpenters and no lime for mortar. The convict James Blodworth was both architect and master builder. He ordered the female convicts to gather shells from Bennelong Point which were then burnt to provide lime which cracked badly and led to many problems with the building years later. Norfolk Island pine was used for some of the interior woodwork and bricks and tiles were made at the brickfields and hauled into town on the convict carts. The house had the first staircase ever built in Australia and terrified the Aboriginals when they first saw a man appear at the upstairs windows. These were the first glazed windows in Australia, since the First Fleet had safely transported over a thousand panes of glass through storm and high seas for this purpose.

On Easter Monday 1789 Governor Phillip left his tiny canvas hut and moved into the first Government House, which stood on land that sloped down to the edge of today's Circular Quay. Its rear boundaries were today's Phillip, Bent and Young Streets, while the house itself stood at the corner of Bridge and Phillip Streets. This small Georgian house drawn by Lieutenant Bradley, who must have visited it frequently, became the centre of the administration and limited social life of Sydney.

By 1790 with the arrival of the Second Fleet, Sydney was desperately short of food and a dinner invitation to Government House meant that guests provided the food for their own meal. Some officers as a joke even arrived with loaves of bread impaled on their swords, announcing that "the staff of life was on the point of death." But a year later Bradley's drawing shows that a large vegetable garden with a barn for storage of crops and vegetables had been made beside the house. Sentries guarded against theft and subsequent paintings of Government House show that the sentry box on the right was still in position some fifty-six years later.

In front of the Government Wharf, which was near today's Customs House at Circular Quay, was a flagstaff flying the Union Flag, made up of the red cross of St. George for England and the Scottish white cross of St. Andrew. St. Patrick's red cross which turned the flag into the Union Jack was only added ten years later. To the left of the Government Wharf was the Governor's boathouse with his own long-boat slung from the rafters.

Captain Phillip left Sydney in December 1792 and a military instead of a naval administration took over, first under Major Grose and in 1794 under Captain Patterson. They both had comfortable homes of their own and Government House lay empty and unattended awaiting the arrival of Governor John Hunter. Phillip was the only Governor who did not complain bitterly about Sydney's Government House but since he had suffered nearly a year in a damp and leaky canvas hut, it must have seemed a great improvement. Subsequent Governors were all disappointed by the state of their residence and spent much of their time doing what they could to alter it from a rustic farmhouse into their idea of an antipodean Vice-Regal residence, and their bitter and frustrated despatches to London make interesting reading.

Governor Hunter, a bachelor who was a keen naturalist, writer and artist of some considerable skill, spent his time building a comfortable residence at Parramatta to hide away from Sydney and the troublesome officers of the Rum Corps. Of his Government House he observed "he could not have had less comfort, although he would have had greater peace of mind, had he spent the time in a penitentiary."

He was replaced in 1800 by Governor Philip Gidley King accompanied by his wife and young family, who needed more space than the bachelor Governors Phillip and Hunter. King found the woodwork eaten away by white ants and dry rot and complained bitterly that "the Government House in Sydney is not habitable until newly roofed and the rotten doors and window frames replaced." George Evans' painting shows the new wing King built to give an additional drawing room and he also added the enormous water tank to the left of the house. At this time there was no piped water in Sydney and the water from the Tank Stream was becoming polluted.

King was replaced by Governor Bligh, already famous for his part in the Bounty mutiny. He was accompanied by his daughter Mary, and her husband, Lieutenant Putland. He took a look at the crumbling woodwork and mortar and the holes in the roof and sent off a characteristically terse but authoritative despatch to London. "Government House wants new doors, windows, shutters, shingles, flooring, white washing and plastering. All in rotten state, wants to be new." His Governorship was a series of stormy confrontations with the officers of the Rum Corps, culminating in the drama of the Rum Rebellion, when Major Johnston and the officers of the Corps stormed into Government House with drawn bayonets just as Bligh and his invited guests including Robert Campbell and John Palmer were at dinner. While Mary Putland screamed insults at the intruders, Bligh was busy hiding confidential documents and the Governor's seal under a bed in a back bedroom. The irascible but courageous Bligh suffered the accusations of cowardice that he had been caught hiding under the bed, but was unable to defend himself. He was held prisoner in his own Government House for a year while first Johnston and then Foveaux took over the running of the Colony. They both had their own homes and neither lived at Government House. In a period of such political upheaval the last thing that anyone thought about was domestic maintenance of an empty Government House. George William Evans' drawing was probably made just before Macquarie was due to arrive as Governor.

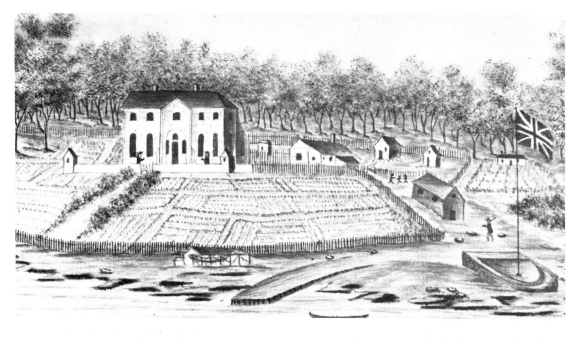

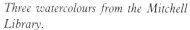

Three watercolours from the Mitchell Library.

Plate 52
Top. WILLIAM BRADLEY. 1791. Governor Arthur Phillip's old prefabricated house with its long sloping roof stands to the right of the two-storey Government House.

Plate 53
Middle. GEORGE W. EVANS. 1808–10. A verandah, another wing and a water storage tank have been added by Governor King.

Plate 54
Bottom. CHARLES RODIUS, 1836. Rodius shows the many additions by different Governors. By 1836 the woodwork was badly eaten away by white ants and Governor Bourke spent as much time as possible at Parramatta, complaining that the Sydney house smelt with dry rot and leaked beyond repair.

Macquarie had been Military Secretary to the Governor of Bombay and was accustomed to the Vice-Regal palaces of India, complete with retinues of well-trained servants. Instead he was confronted by a crumbling farmhouse with a cabbage garden outside the door and some relatively untrained convict servants. "No private gentleman in the Colony is so ill-accommodated as I am" he wrote. But, as a practical administrator, he was more immediately concerned with lack of adequate hospital facilities, poor accommodation for his soldiers, the robberies and outrages committed by convicts who wandered the streets at night and the safety of precious government supplies.

So he concentrated his efforts on building a new hosptial, Military and Convict Barracks and a Commissariat Stores. Government House he considered "in such a decayed and ruinous state from white ants having got into the timber that it will tumble down of itself in a few years." Phillip's original gabled home, now used as the Governor's office was "so decayed and rotten as to be unsafe" and the kitchens "in a most ruinous State." He recommended building a completely new Government House on the site of Boston's old windmill "in the new castellated style," and forcibly repossessed the site of the windmill from John Palmer.

London remained silent concerning a new Government House, so he and his wife added two new bedrooms and a new dining room to the Sydney house. Mrs Macquarie ordered the removal of the vegetable patch which was replaced by a garden, landscaped in the latest picturesque style, complete with shrubs, Norfolk pine trees, gently sloping lawns and tame wallabies to complete the exotic note.

At the beginning of 1820, having previously entertained Captain and Mrs de Freycinet at Old Government House, Parramatta, the Macquaries entertained them for a farewell visit in Sydney. Having heard tales of woe concerning Sydney's Government House, Captain and Mme. de Freycinet were agreeably surprised.

They described how "the building is not beautiful due to its irregularity, but the inside is handsomer than one would expect from the house's lack of symmetry." These remarks were compliments to the good taste of the Macquaries, since the de Freycinets were an aristocratic young couple who were accustomed to elegant chateaux and manor houses in France. They were particularly impressed with the Governor's stables which had just been completed and on sailing up the harbour had been convinced, like many other foreign ships, that these handsome stables must be the Governor's residence.

It was these same stables that were to cause so much trouble and act as a nail in the coffin of Macquarie's career as Governor. Early in 1819 Macquarie informed Colonial Secretary Bathurst that "I have long suffered such very great inconvenience from the want of secure stables for my horses and decent sleeping places for my servants" and described the stables that were currently being built as "commodious though not expensive." However Macquarie obviously failed to communicate this concept to Francis Greenway, his talented but fiery architect with the fertile imagination.

Greenway was determined that these Governor's stables should blend harmoniously with the proposed "castellated" new Government House to be built alongside them. Accordingly he used the finest materials and stone to built on the site of the old Government bakery,

within full view of the proposed site of the house, stabling for thirty horses designed as a small replica of Inverary Castle. This was a great mediaeval Gothic revival building by a Macquarie kinsman, the Duke of Argyle. Greenway designed his proposed Government House as a majestic version of the stables but fate was to intervene in the shape of Commissioner Bigge.

While the stables were still under construction Bigge arrived, sent out from London by Lord Bathurst to report on Macquarie's expenditure and building programme. He wrote a bitter attack on Macquarie's extravagant buildings, as unsuitable for a struggling convict colony and citied the stables as an example. These he considered far exceeded the wants or allowance of any Governor. Macquarie was reprimanded and informed that all his future building plans must be submitted to the Treasury for prior sanction. Macquarie, by this time overworked, ill and worried about his forthcoming retirement and pension prospects, replied that in that case he would leave the building of a new Government House to his successor. He had tried from the outset to turn Sydney into a dignified city rather than a tumble-down convict colony and must have felt keenly the lack of appreciation for his endeavours. So after more than eleven years as Governor, he decided to retire.

He was replaced by Sir Thomas Brisbane who took over the thankless task in December 1821. He considered Sydney's Government House unfit for a Governor's residence and spent his time at Old Government House, Parramatta, where he built a large observatory and spent happy hours cataloguing the stars. Brisbane, as a highly-intelligent scientist had many plans for the improvement of the colony but he made the mistake of living out at Parramatta and leaving their execution to the overbearing and bungling Major Goulburn. His most important plan that was implemented was contained in a despatch to Lord Bathurst when he suggested the development of Circular Quay, writing that "it would be highly desirable to sell or let on building leases the whole of the waterside of the Government Domain ... for the erection of Quays, Stores and Warehouses." He further suggested that new Government House could be built with the money so obtained or that the funds should be used to convert Greenway's government stables into the proposed Government House. However, nothing came of his suggestion and, in 1821, Thomas Brisbane sailed away from Sydney and the problems of its Government House, a disappointed and disillusioned ex-Governor.

Brisbane was not replaced until 1825 by Lieutenant-General Sir Ralph Darling, who was also used to the luxurious Vice-Regal palaces of India and the handsome Governor's Residence in Mauritius, where he had spent eighteen months as Acting-Governor. He arrived expecting the worst about the state of Sydney's Government House since he had received a verbal promise from the Colonial Office to build a new Vice-Regal residence. However, on his arrival with his wife and young family, he was strongly advised that it would be disastrous to build without letting the timber dry out for two years in advance. He too used Government House, Sydney, for formal entertaining and tried to spend as much time as possible at the more comfortable residence at Parramatta. In spite of considerable health problems, he and his wife tried to do what they could to make the dilapidated old house into a suitable social venue for the growing colony. However, he fell out with Wentworth and other influential members of Sydney's society and towards the end of his Governorship, many people flatly refused to attend functions at Government House or even invite the Darlings to social events.

Augustus Earle considered Government House a "mean and unpretentious building" when he drew Governor Darling and his wife walking in the gardens that were tended by convicts. The French naval artist, Louis de Sainson together with the leader of the French scientific expedition, the French nobleman Jules Cesar Dumont d'Urville were also entertained at Government House by the Darlings. Dumont d'Urville was a French nobleman in command of an expedition under French royal patronage, designed to obtain both scientific knowledge and international prestige for France. They were sent by the French king to explore and chart new areas of the world from the ship *Astrolabe* in much the same way as space explorers are employed today. The expedition was also searching for clues concerning the fate of La Perouse, France's equivalent of Captain Cook, who had disappeared in the South Seas.

Both Dumont d'Urville's expedition and the ship that brought the artist Duperrey to Sydney in 1824 were convinced on their first sight of Sydney Cove that the magnificent stables must be the residence of the Governor and not of his horses. When de Sainson made his drawing the stables were surrounded by trees and parklands and he described them as resembling a crusader's castle. Today the crusader's castle sits marooned by a motorway as one of the world's most unusual Conservatoriums of Music. Personal tragedy also struck the Darlings at Government House, Sydney. Like Mrs Macquarie, Mrs Darling

gave birth to a much wanted son, who died after eight months and she was depressed for many months afterwards. Darling's governorship politically went from bad to worse, he made numerous enemies and as the Darlings sailed away on 21st October, 1831, they must have been glad to leave their unhappy Sydney residence.

The next Governor was to find Government House "unhealthy as well as inconvenient." Major-General Sir Richard Bourke was a capable administrator and a qualified barrister.

A member of the Irish landed gentry, he was the first Governor with practical experience of running his own large property. This was his second Governorship and he was used to the luxurious Government House at the Cape Colony. However on arrival his wife was seriously ill, and horrified by the state of the Sydney residence, they preferred to live quietly at Old Government House. The following year she died there.

Bourke went into mourning and continued to live at Parramatta. However, six months after his wife's death he wrote a thoughtful and informative report to London strongly recommending Brisbane's plan of selling off the land that is now Circular Quay East to finance the building of the new Government House. He called the Sydney residence "a collection of Rooms built at different times by different Governors ... which are inconvenient and unsightly. The roof and flooring are decayed and the bad smells, which prevail in the principal Sitting Room are not only unpleasant but unhealthy. The house ... has now reached a state of Deterioration in which it would be a Waste of Money to spend a large sum for its preservation." However the house was to continue as the Governor's Residence for another eleven years.

Plate 55

LOUIS DE SAINSON. **The Governor's Stables.** *Lithograph from DUMONT D'URVILLE'S "Voyage de la Corvette l'Astrolabe" 1826. □ These handsome stables designed by Francis Greenway originally housed 24 mares and the stallions were stabled in the octagonal towers. There were also offices for the Governor's staff. From the harbour the stables looked far more imposing than Government House and visitors were always surprised to find that this building was not the Governor's Residence but that of his horses. Today the drive and trees have vanished under the Cahill Expressway and the stables are now the Conservatorium of Music.*

Bourke was finally successful in securing approval to build a new residence, but London retaliated with the order that as soon as the new Government House was built Old Government House, Parramatta "should be disposed of, in the most advantageous manner."

In 1836 a committee was formed to plan the new residence, composed of Alexander Berry, Hannibal Macarthur, Major George Barney as Civil Engineer and Mortimer Lewis as the official architect. After several changes of plan, they decided that it would be impossible to build on the site of Boston's Mill as "the present Stables would completely overpower the new House" and that to re-establish new stables after demolishing Greenway's would be far too expensive. They chose the present site of Government House for its privacy and harbour views. The committee obtained the sanction of the Colonial Office to extend Macquarie and Phillip Streets down through the Domain lands to Major Barney's Semi-Circular Quay, on which work had already commenced. By this time, the estimates for building the new residence were more than double Darling's original costings.

The following year the *Herald* demanded rather peevishly "What does Bourke want with two establishments? If the Governor wants a country residence, he ought to pay for it himself." By this time Bourke had quarrelled bitterly with Campbell Drummond Riddell, his avaricious Scottish Treasurer. Public insults were exchanged and Bourke requested his Treasurer's dismissal by the Colonial Office in London.

The issue was complex and involved various fine points of constitutional law. Glenelg, the Colonial Secretary, chose to support his fellow Scot, Drummond Riddell, against Bourke, who felt that since Glenelg had failed to support his authority as Governor he had no option other than to resign. The colony erected a statue to the Governor who had instituted great reforms to the electoral, legal and educational systems and greatly improved the treatment of convicts, free settlers and emancipists.

Sadly Bourke never saw the completion of the new Government House, which he had spent hours planning, but at least the foundations had been laid. His statue originally looked out over the Government House to which he had devoted so much energy but, with the advent of the Cahill Expressway, it was moved to its present position close to the Mitchell Library.

Plate 56
AUGUSTUS EARLE. **Government House and Gardens.** *Lithograph from Earle's "Views in New South Wales and Tasmania," published 1830. □ Governor and Mrs Darling admire the gardens, while a convict in his leather hat rolls the immaculate pathways designed by Mrs Macquarie. Once the present Government House was built, the grounds west of Macquarie Street were sold off to finance the building of Circular Quay.*

Bourke was replaced in 1837 by Sir George Gipps, the last Governor to reside in the old house. A painting made by convict artist George Peacock in 1845 as Gipps moved out officially shows Government House with holes in the roof and overgrown lawns, but in fact he had fled to his new home many months previously. The picture shows a flock of sheep and somewhat surprisingly two camels grazing on the once-immaculate lawns, since the land had been let to a farmer while the planned extensons of Bridge and Macquarie Streets were carried out. A short lease was also offered for rental of the decaying house but there were no suitable applicants and it was gradually dismantled. Towards the end of Gipps' residence the condition of the house was so dangerous with rot that the Queen's Birthday Ball was held in the partly-completed Government House before its official opening two years later in 1845.

So Gipps actually moved into his new Government House before it was completely ready. In a wonderful piece of inspired lunacy, convicts from the Hyde Park Barracks were used as removal men to save funds. Not surprisingly, on the night of the move, silver and jewellery were found to be missing and a search revealed the missing valuables were concealed in the prisoners' dormitories of the convict Barracks. The old and historic house which had witnessed so much frustration on the part of nine governors over half a century was gradually demolished and its stones used to build the approaches to the Quay.

In 1846 Gipps retired due to overwork and ill-health and was replaced by the aristocratic sportsman, Sir Charles FitzRoy. He was the grandson of one Royal Duke and was married to the eldest daughter of another. He had a wandering eye for the ladies and his long-suffering wife was sharply criticised by the *Herald* the following year for failing to include the younger and prettier ladies of Sydney on her invitation list. She departed to Parramatta for a long holiday and FitzRoy promptly invited all the younger ladies plus some ladies of dubious virtue to his official reception and was severely criticised again.

Irked by so much criticism, he spent more and more time at Old Government House, Parramatta, where he had built large kennels to house his pack of imported foxhounds to hunt dingos and kangaroos. Used to the great ducal country houses of Britain, he much preferred the sporting life and enjoyed hunting in the park at Parramatta.

When criticised over the expense of maintaining two Government Houses, he retorted haughtily that he would personally pay for the upkeep of Old Government House but was surprised that anyone should "interfere with the private arrangements of the Governor." On 7th December, 1847 tragedy occurred in the park. FitzRoy enjoyed driving his own thoroughbred horses and had already had several minor accidents through driving too fast. The Governor and his wife, Lady Mary, were leaving Old Government House for a wedding when the horses took fright and bolted. The carriage overturned and Lady Mary was flung out against a tree and died in agony in her husband's arms. FitzRoy himself was crippled for several months. Much of his popularity as Governor had been due to Lady Mary's charm and social skill and FitzRoy had relied on her as an official hostess, confidante and loyal companion. FitzRoy was depressed for many months after

Plate 57
THOMAS WATLING. **The first residence of Governor Phillip at Parramatta about 1794.** ☐
Published as an illustration to Judge Advocate David Collins' "An Account of the English Colony in New South Wales." Watling worked as an assigned convict for Collins but received no acknowledgement for the drawing that he made and Collins published. It shows the little residence whose roof finally fell in. It also gives a clear picture of the building methods used by the convicts of the First Fleet and shows the stocks, used as a place of punishment. It is interesting that Governor Phillip had no hipped roof or verandah to protect his residence from sun and storm.

*Plate 58   GEORGE WILLIAM EVANS. **Old Government House, Parramatta.** Undated watercolour,
c.1808-9. □ The well-known surveyor and explorer shows the small Georgian residence built by
Governor Hunter with a rustic trellis around the front door and a pavilion beside the house. In the same
way as she redesigned the Sydney garden, Mrs Macquarie appears to have ordered the removal of the
vegetable garden and the picket fence and turned the area into a park. Mitchell Library.*

the accident, and he lost his enthusiasm for the sporting life at Old
Government House and for the rest of his Governorship spent little
time there.

Sir William Dennison had ten children and a limited income. He
had problems enough with the Sydney Government House which had
suffered without the capable Lady Mary FitzRoy in charge. He found
the house "full of bugs" the mortar was cracking in several places and
the gas leaked.

The very limited laundry facilities were inadequate to deal with
washing for ten children and until an adequate laundry was built, the
Dennison family laundry was sent out by horse and cart to be washed
at Old Government House.

Dennison reported that Old Government House was "in a miserable state, with white ants in the rafters and roof shingles" and rather
than pay for repairs out of his own purse or face another series of
lengthy confrontations with the Colonial Office, he decided to abandon the house.

The contents were sold at auction, the land around the house was
proclaimed a public park and the house was let to a series of tenants. In
1909 it was leased to the King's School, Parramatta, and at the
expiration of the lease the house came under the control of the
National Trust which has extensively restored the building and discovered the foundations of the original homes built by Governor Phillip
and Governor Hunter. Watling's drawing shows the house built by
Governor Phillip in 1790, surrounded by convicts' wattle and daub
cottages and a large vegetable garden. The stocks are situated on the
right of the approach to the house, where offenders were immobilised
by the ankles while being pelted with refuse. The beams of the house
were eaten away by white ants and by 1799 when Governor Hunter
arrived, the roof had fallen in. He built the small Georgian manor
house with the rustic trellis work round the front door that was painted
by surveyor George William Evans.

Both Hunter and the Macquaries enjoyed spending their free time
and holidays at Parramatta. Macquarie commissioned his aide-de-
camp, John Watts, who had previously trained as an architect, to
enlarge Hunter's house and the little summer pavilion on the right was
replaced by two wings in the elegant Palladian style, connected to the
main house by colonnades.

72

Plate 59   *JACQUES ARAGO.* **Old Government House in 1818,** *published 1826. ☐ Redrawn for engraving by Marchais and published in Captain Louis de Freycinet's "Voyage autour du Monde," it shows the visit made by Captain and Mme. de Freycinet to Governor and Mrs Macquarie at the end of 1818. The engraving shows Lieutenant Watts' additions to the house, the handsome portico designed by Greenway and the new park. Dixson Library.*

The picket fence and the vegetable garden were removed and it is easy to see why so many Governors preferred to spend as much of their time as possible here to escape from the evil smells and discomfort of the Government House on today's Bridge Street.

In 1820 another disaster was narrowly averted when Old Government House was struck "by an electric fireball." Doors were pulled off their frames by the force of the lightning, several windows were broken and "the house was full of the suffocating smell of sulphur as a result of the bursting of the immense ball of fire," which also destroyed one wall. Macquarie was away on an official tour and Mrs Macquarie and her only son were in the only wing "not visited by the scourge and to this may be attributed their almost miraculous escape."

A portico was commissioned by Macquarie from Francis Greenway. Shortly after completion it appeared in the centre of the handsome copper engraving which illustrated Captain Louis de Freycinet's account of his voyage around the world in the *Uranie.* Also aboard was a young naval lieutenant named Jacques Arago, who wrote a series of amusing letters to his brother in France about his experiences in Australia and the paintings he had made. The engraving closely resembles the style of Arago's other paintings. Arago, an aristocratic and charming young man was widely entertained by members of Sydney society like "Monsieur Woolstoncroft, Monsieur Piper at his chateau and Monsieur le Baron Field," and the Macquaries. The most vivid account of the day's outing was provided by the young Rose de Freycinet, who also kept a journal. She described how the official Government Barge brought them up the Parramatta River, while another followed with a regimental band playing water-music. Mrs Macquarie was "a charming women of conspicuous ability" and Old Government House "displayed the simple elegance that the English know so well how to create wherever they are."

Arago's drawing shows the de Freycinets welcomed at the front porch of Old Government House, which with its elegant Georgian proportions and fine furniture was obviously more suitable for the entertainment of official guests than Government House Sydney.

A visit to this beautiful house today shows how the National Trust has succeeded in preserving the elegance and charm of Australia's earliest surviving public building.

The New Government House

Edward Blore extended Buckingham Palace for Queen Victoria's expanding family and made some sympathetic renovations to mediaeval Windsor Castle and Tudor Hampton Court. His acceptance of the architect's brief for Sydney's new Victorian Tudor Gothic Government House gave a sense of prestige to the whole Colony. Since he was the highly fashionable Royal Architect, his services were much in demand. It was impossible for him to undertake the long voyage to Australia, so he never saw "the superlatively castellated, crenellated and turreted Vice-Regal residence" that he had designed. Mortimer Lewis and George Barney provided the necessary local knowledge to rearrange some of the main rooms to obtain the best harbour views and supervised the builders. Cedar was shipped from the Shoalhaven and Hunter Rivers and stone was specially quarried at Pyrmont. Marble was brought to the Domain by bullock-waggon from some of Australia's finest quarries. There were extensive cellars, the ground floor had twelve public rooms and the first floor thirteen bedrooms and there were enormous staff quarters connected by winding passageways. With its crenellated battlements, turrets, mullioned windows and heraldic stone carvings, the new house expressed all the romanticism of the Victorian age.

The castellated house originally required by Macquarie had taken nearly 30 years to build and was now the talk of Sydney. The Royal Architect had personally recreated this baronial Tudor castle and now here it was, on view for the first time, surrounded by gum trees and emus at the edge of Farm Cove. Gipps, never one of Sydney's most popular Governors, found his invitations to the offical opening on 26th June 1845 were eagerly accepted by those who wished to see the interior of a Government House that was now the height of fashion. Greenway's much maligned Government Stables blended superbly with the new house. Within a few years "castellated mansions like Carthona, Lindesay, Vaucluse, Greenoaks, The Rangers, The Hermitage and Grantham" had taken over some of the most commanding situations around the Harbour. Those who wished to be fashionable but could not afford to re-build in the new style hastily ordered Gothic wallpaper, Gothic bookcases, high-backed velvet-seated Gothic dining chairs, massive monastic oak dining tables and inserted marble fireplaces complete with heraldic shields. More mediaeval furniture must have been carved during the mid-Victorian period than during the entire middle ages.

The newspapers and guide books of the period were enraptured. At last, instead of a smelly, dilapidated and unfashionable house they had something to describe with pride. "So handsome a structure reminds the traveller of the castellated palaces of ancient times. May the solidity, the splendour and the elegance of this Vice-Regal mansion be an emblem of Australia's future history," wrote the Sydney press. From London, *The Illustrated News* described it as "a magnificent structure, most elegantly furnished, with heraldic chimney pieces that are splendid specimens of the finest local marble."

The new Residence had a long ballroom complete with mediaeval-style musicians' gallery and a large drawing room with magnificent water views and ceiling painted with Australian native flowers. Pride of place in the dining room went to the portrait of Governor Brisbane by Augustus Earle. By an uncanny and ironic coincidence, Brisbane, the Governor who refused to live at the Sydney residence and shut himself away in the Observatory at Parramatta was painted by Earle against the exact stretch of the harbour looking up to the Heads, that mirrored the view from the windows of the present Government House.

Naturally there were a few critics. Lieutenant-Colonel Mundy, a cousin of Governor FitzRoy, bemoaned the lack of verandahs or window shades against Sydney's semi-tropical summer sun and wrote, "this fault extends even to Government House, whose great staring windows are doomed to grill unveiled" since Blore thought that any projection over their stone mullions would spoil the aesthetic convention of this Gothic castle. Another visitor issued a practical note of warning about the lack of a porch. "The architect possibly considered it unnecessary to provide against wet ... but he had seen the sudden deluges of rain that descend here, instead of the imposing arched entrance, he might have substituted an archway for carriages. In a shower, I fear the ladies will declare him no master of his craft." The visitor, Mr John Hood, was right.

After indignant complaints from ladies who had ruined their silk dancing shoes climbing into their carriages ankle-deep in mud, the deep archway that formed the main door that appears in Joseph Fowles' picture was finally filled in with a window. Below this window was the handsome covered portico or carriage entrance designed by James Barnet who was Colonial Architect. Completed in 1874, it still forms the imposing entrance to Government House today.

Plate 60   *JOSEPH FOWLES.* **Government House c.1845.** *Watercolour. Mitchell Library.* □ *Joseph Fowles was Drawing Master at Sydney Grammar School and the King's School at Parramatta. His detailed and accurate engraved drawings of Sydney were published in 1848 with part of this view engraved as the frontispiece. He said that his aims were "to remove erroneous and discreditable notions concerning this city and . . . to show its public edifices . . . and its beautiful and commodious buildings.*

His painting shows a mid-Victorian romantic Gothic castle complete with turrets and battlements, where emus roam free and cavalry officers prance across immaculate lawns, in front of admiring visitors. The great arched entrance to the house was filled in. A covered porchway now provides shelter for the Governor's guests. Fowles himself described Government House as "one of our most imposing buildings" and featured it as the frontispiece of his Sydney book, which he diplomatically dedicated to Governor FitzRoy. The book became a best-seller, was re-issued in three separate editions, and is still the classic reference work on early Victorian and late Georgian Sydney."

Plate 61
JOHN CLARKE HOYTE. **The Burning of the Garden Palace, seen from the North Shore**
Watercolour by New Zealand artist J. C. Hoyte who was living at Mosman at the time of the fire on 22nd September, 1882, this painting is today preserved in the Mitchell Library. □

The vast Garden Palace of glass and brick was built facing Macquarie Street along the Inner Domain for the International Exhibition of 1879-1880. When burnt down after only three years it contained a number of valuable museum collections awaiting permanent homes, including the whole of the Technological Museum, the specimens of the Mining Museum and an exhibition of 300 paintings organised by the Art Society of New South Wales.

The artists were practically the only people who benefited from the blaze. Their pictures had all been insured and several Australian artists were subsequently able to afford a trip overseas on the benefits of their large insurance pay-outs.

The magnificent Garden Palace went up like a tinder-box. It had been constructed very hurriedly using a thin wooden framework covered by an iron skin and it was never intended for permanent use, although the New South Wales Government had planned to use the Palace as a show piece for Australia's first centenary celebrations in 1888.

The fire began just as the night and day watchmen were changing their shifts. No satisfactory explanation was ever found for the cause of the blaze.

Plate 62 **The Garden Palace,** *home of Australia's first International Exhibition, which was attended by more than one million people.* ☐ *This wood engraving was made for a special commemorative supplement of the Illustrated Sydney News for the opening of the great palace. The Garden Palace had a huge central dome somewhat similar to a design by Sir Christopher Wren. Each State in Australia had its own Exhibition Pavilion, resplendent with the finest examples of its agricultural produce and wines and choice examples of craftsmanship surrounded by massed banks of ferns and aspidistras. Overseas exhibitors like Royal Doulton sent large collections of specially made porcelain.*

The Burning of the Garden Palace

The *Sydney Morning Herald* for Saturday, 23rd September 1882 ran banner headlines with an eye-witness account of the most spectacular fire ever seen in Australia. Their reporter said "The whole of the Australian colonies and we might add, the whole of the civilised world, will hear with regret that the Garden Palace was yesterday totally destroyed by fire. This grand edifice designed by Mr James Barnet, the Colonial Architect, which will be remembered by exhibitors and visitors from all over the world . . . was erected in a remarkably short space of time, like the fabled palace of Aladdin in the Arabian Nights.

The actual commencement of building took place on 13th January, 1879 and exactly eight months afterwards the building was finished and the Exhibition opened. Portions of the building have been used for concerts, oratorios, balls and public meetings. The Galleries were devoted to purposes such as Museums and Lecture Rooms. Whether it was well to use a building constructed entirely of timber for the storage of public records may be questioned . . . In less than an hour yesterday morning the whole edifice with its contents was totally destroyed, leaving only a few crumbling brick piers and smoking cinders to mark the spot where stood one of the most graceful structures to be found south of the Equator.

The flames burst throught the dome, then to the right and left, the roofing like a gigantic firework breaking into dotted lines of light. The flames appeared to run along the interior walls before they broke out, as in places great gaps were left between outbursts. Reaching the towers the fire rippled along their parapets and within a few minutes there was no point of the building that was not fringed with bright flames. Then came a dull roaring and crackling like the discharge of firearms . . . volumes of black smoke rolled up and, with a crash like a peal of thunder, the whole mighty dome fell in. The current of air created by its fall carried up in the whirlwind great sheets of galvanised iron and burning embers. The wind carried the iron and fragments of the dome far away to the suburbs . . . of Rushcutters Bay, Potts Point and Darling Point. Two sheets of corrugated iron fell into the grounds of the Hon. William Macleay at Elizabeth Bay.

The flames were sometimes tempered with carmine, red, green, yellow or blue by the burning of the galvanised roofing and the heat was so great that at six o'clock (in the morning), the glass in the windows of houses in Macquarie Street began to crack. The high-balconied houses in Macquarie Street presented a carnival appearance, with spectators even on the tops of the houses.

When the fire was raging in its greatest strength, the sun was seen behind the burning Palace, rising above the horizon in a crimson disc. The scene was the most imposing and yet the most pitiful ever seen in the Colonies. The breeze blowing towards that direction, it was feared that the Art Gallery might be endangered and firemen were stationed in its locality, but fortunately their services were not required. It is to be hoped that the lesson of yesterday will have at least this fruit, that our Colony's collection of pictures will be placed in a substantial building, and no longer left to share the fate of the works of art in our Garden Palace. The fire was now in the fullness of its power, walls were falling, towers toppling over and tumbling, huge masses of ruin into the great lustrous sea of red-hot metal and burning woodwork beneath. By nine o'clock all was over, the residences of Macquarie Street had their view of the Harbour restored to them and the pretty Garden Palace was a mass of smoking timbers and falling walls.

A very large number of works of art, purchased by the Government and placed in the Garden Palace were also destroyed. Some of them are not to be regretted, but others were very fine and the collection cost the Colony a large sum of money. The Art Society of New South Wales was to have held its Annual Exhibition on the 2nd October in the Garden Palace. About 300 pictures had been sent in and the Hanging Committee, Messrs A. Collingridge, W. C. Piguenit, J. C. Hoyte and W. C. Smedley had hung the pictures. Mr E. Coombs, President of the Art Society lost twelve pictures and a wonderful teak mantelpiece. Mr J. C. Hoyte, the Vice-President of the Society lost several, Messrs. Collingridge lost a large number including "Her Majesty's Mail — Stuck Up." . . .

It was a fortunate and almost a marvellous circumstance that the Art Gallery with its treasures was not consumed and the destruction of the Garden Palace only emphasises the recommendation made over and over again, that the pictures, statues and ceramic ware should be placed where they have a better chance of preservation."

John Boston's Windmill

This stone windmill towered over the Sydney skyline for over 40 years, it belonged to John Boston, surgeon, entrepreneur and freebooting adventurer, who became Australia's first defender of civil rights and lived a life as colourful as any swashbuckling film hero.

Boston was a trained surgeon but, at the time of the First Fleet, surgery was not the prosperous career it is today. Prior to the discoveries of ether and chloroform in the 1840s, the prospect of intense pain often made even death seem preferable to surgery, so surgeons often looked for alternative means of supplementing their incomes. The radical young Boston was attracted by the idea of travelling around the world. In 1793 he wrote to the Colonial Secretary offering his services in Sydney not as a surgeon but for his knowledge of "brewing, distilling, curing fish, vinegar and soap making," since at university he had specialised in pharmacy. The idea of a fish smoking plant in Sydney sounded an attractive financial export proposition to the Colonial Office, and he became Australia's third free settler. He was allowed to lease part of The Domain from Commissary John Palmer for this purpose. The smoked fish went bad, but the ingenious Boston tried panning salt, using sand from Bennelong Point. This also failed and Boston's commercial prospects looked distinctly poor. However, at the end of 1794 he built this enormous stone windmill on the Domain land at a time when owning a windmill was highly lucrative, since every Sydney dweller needed to have his flour ration ground for bread, and some convicts had been known to queue all night to use a mill. Boston also ground Indian corn or maize for convict porridge. Reading through an old encyclopaedia gave him the idea of brewing beer using the remains of the maize. To make it bitter he used the stalks of Cape gooseberries since he had no hops and so became one of Australia's first commercial brewers. Around the base of the mill Boston kept pigs which involved him in the lawsuit that was to make him famous in Sydney for many years as a champion of the underdog.

Quartermaster Laycock, a powerful member of the Rum Corps harboured a grudge against Boston. Finding one of Boston's pigs, just about to give birth to a litter of piglets, Laycock ordered a soldier to shoot the pig for trespassing on military property. Boston appeared, harsh words were exchanged and Boston was beaten up by the bully boys of the New South Wales Corps on Laycock's orders. Boston took the case to court, the first man ever to sue the military authorities. The trial lasted seven days and aroused the intense interest of the entire civilian community, Boston was accused of being a revolutionary, who had "drunk damnation to the King of England and all the crowned heads of Europe" and a man unsuitable to stay in the Colony. The talented Boston conducted his own defence and, amid great rejoicing by the civilians, won his case but was awarded only a tiny fraction of the high damages he had claimed.

In 1802 Boston and Simeon Lord purchased a wrecked Spanish sailing vessel. They towed it to Sydney and repaired it. Boston invested all his capital in a cargo of sealskins and whale oil which he intended to trade at Cape of Good Hope for goods for the Sydney market. The ship *La Pluma*, Spanish for feather, behaved just like one, was blown off course and ended up a total wreck this time on a reef off the Philippines.

The versatile Boston persuaded the Spanish to let him start a distillery in Manila, which he then sold for enought profit to purchase an American ship in which to return to Sydney. On his return he found that James Squire was making better and more popular beer from genuine hops at his Kissing Point brewery and that more windmills had sprung up in competition around Sydney.

Boston decided his future lay as a trader and adventurer on the high seas. He purchased a cargo of 14,000 sealskins jointly with Simeon Lord as a sleeping partner and in 1804 set off in his new ship for America, aiming to collect additional cargo from several islands in the South Seas. He made the fatal error of landing on Tongatapu in the Tongan or Friendly Islands group. The islanders were not as friendly as their name and, as Boston and his companions stepped ashore, they were all murdered.

The mill still continued to be known as Boston's Mill, to distinguish it from the other Sydney landmark, Palmer's Mill. As Russell's drawing shows, it was built on high ground just above today's Conservatorium whose towers appear in the picture. The land had one of the best views in Sydney and was wanted by Macquarie as the site for Government House. James Meehan's 1807 map shows Boston's and Palmer's Mills, with the message "Land necessary for the building of New Government House but Leases improperly granted" beside them. Eventually Macquarie resumed the land and partially demolished Boston's Mill, but by then the age of the gigantic windmills of Sydney was drawing to a close. In 1815 engineer John Dickson introduced the industrial revolution to Australia at his yard in Darlinghurst, when he demonstrated his steam-powered mill, which crushed 260 bushels of grain a day, compared to the 12 bushels crushed by the average windmill. By the time Russell drew the great mill it was silent, with its sails rotted away.

Robert Russell himself was both a surveyor and architect. He had worked for the celebrated John Nash, the elegant and classical London architect, famous for his designs of the Nash terraces of Regent's Park and Regent Street's sweeping arcades, when Nash was converting Buckingham House into a royal palace for George IV. This work gave Russell an eye for line and form which was to echo throughout his drawings of Australia's unique adaptations of Georgian architecture, and perhaps accounts for his fascination with Greenway's elegant buildings.

The Sketches of Robert Russell

Russell wished to travel around the world and, like Martens, he ended up in Sydney with an introduction to Sir Thomas Mitchell. Mitchell was delighted to employ someone with Russell's experience and immediately appointed him as Assistant Surveyor of Sydney, working on George Street North. Russell became a close friend of Conrad Martens, and one of his first pupils and patrons, and the two men were to remain friends for the rest of their lives. Russell had a great admiration for the work of Martens, Turner and Girtin and he gradually built up a fine collection of their watercolours and drawings. He was also a competent etcher and lithographer. The drawings from his Sydney sketchbook were printed for him by John Austin, on the lithograph press Austin bought from the artist Augustus Earle. This press had been brought to Australia by Governor Brisbane and Austin's printing services were obviously in demand, since for a time it was the only lithograph press in commercial hands in Sydney. Russell's edition of the best of his Sydney drawings was published in 1836, three years after he arrived in Sydney.

In many of his drawings the convict builders of Sydney appear, plodding slowly back to the Barracks after a hard day's work, wearing their black leather hats and carrying their picks and shovels. Unlike many artists, who chose to ignore this aspect of Sydney in favour of the picturesque, a compassionate Russell saw the tragedy of these lonely men, who were forced to build their own jail around them to obtain their freedom.

In September 1836 Russell was promoted to Surveyor of the new Port Phillip settlement but his public service career was stormy and in 1839 he was removed from office and replaced by Robert Hoddle. Russell then went into private practice as an architect and worked on some of Melbourne's most important early buildings. From 1856-1860 he travelled around England and Europe as an exclusive and expensive private guide for wealthy Australian graziers, who wished to visit the major works in art galleries accompanied by their own personal art expert.

He died in Melbourne in 1890, but Sydney owes him an enormous debt for recording so many of the city's important Georgian buildings.

Plate 63
*ROBERT RUSSELL. **The ruins of John Boston's Windmill in the Domain, with the Government Stables (today's Conservatorium) on left. (detail) 1836.** Lithograph. Mitchell Library.*

Fort Macquarie

Plate 64
ROBERT RUSSELL. **Fort Macquarie,
1836.** *Lithograph. Mitchell Library, Sydney
(Q981.1A/p.16).*

It is hard today to look at the soaring sails of the Opera House and imagine instead the towers of Fort Macquarie rising out of the water against the same sky. But during the nineteenth century, one of Sydney's favourite Sunday walks lay past the wool clippers of the Semi-Circular Quay to Fort Macquarie. In 1817 Macquarie wrote to Colonial Secretary Lord Bathurst explaining that he intended to build "a small Fort for the purpose of preventing ships . . . leaving the Cove without permission . . . to be built entirely by Government labourers," and using Government or convict labour ensured that the extensive work necessary to quarry down the Tarpeian Rock, the large stone outcrop on Bennelong point would be very cheap. By the following year this enormous civil engineering project had been completed by convicts using picks and shovels.

Initially the Fort was built on an island off the tip of Bennelong Point and it was reached by a small ornamental drawbridge. But, by the time that Russell drew it, the moat had been filled in using earth and stones obtained from the building of Circular Quay East, designed by Francis Greenway as "a neat but handsome Fort", it was built as a square. Each of the low round towers, lapped by the high tide, had a gun pointing out to sea. The high central Tudor-style tower with the flagstaff was built over a basement containing 350 barrels of gunpowder and all necessary stores for a garrison of 12 soldiers commanded by a sergeant.

During the Crimean War there were fears that the French might try to capture Sydney for a French outpost in the South Seas. The guns of Fort Macquarie must have been comforting for Sydney's inhabitants but they were never to fire a shot in anger. The Fort remained a landmark until 1902. Then, in a piece of inspired civic bathos, the Fort was demolished and a red brick tram depot with mediaeval towers was built on the site, which still continued to be known as Fort Macquarie until it too was demolished to make way for the Opera House.

The South Head Lighthouse

Plate 65
ROBERT RUSSELL. **The South Head or Macquarie Lighthouse in 1836.** *Lithograph from the Mitchell Library.*

In 1816 Governor Macquarie instructed convict architect Francis Greenway to design Australia's first lighthouse, to replace the beacon fire lit on the South Head every night since 1794. Russell drew this simple but beautiful Regency design, built by Greenway from sandstone that he feared was too soft for a tower, but was ordered to use.

Russell's elegant drawing, worthy of his instructor Conrad Martens, shows the twin wings surmounted by domes that gave the lighthouse the charm of a Regency villa at Brighton. Macquarie was aware that his enemies could criticise him for extravagance in building such an elegant lighthouse for a convict colony. To protect himself he insisted that the building should have room for a small military garrison in one domed wing, while lighthouse keeper Robert Watson, after whom Watson's Bay was named, inhabited the other.

The lighthouse took 17 months to build. On 16th December 1817 the Governor and Mrs Macquarie, accompanied by some friends, drove out at dawn "to view this noble, magnificent edifice and take breakfast there." Due to the beauty of his design, Greenway won his freedom from the convict system and Macquarie presented him with a signed convict pardon. The ex-convict could then sit down and join the Vice-Regal breakfast party as a free man. To pay for the maintenance of the oil lamp and its giant lens, all foreign vessels entering the harbour were charged a special levy.

A trip to the lighthouse was a standard nineteenth-century jaunt for overseas visitors. The French naval artist, Louis de Sainson, was so impressed that he made a glamorous drawing of the place in a thunderstorm complete with flashes of lightning. Augustus Earle also painted it in a storm but thought the picture important enough to send to London for exhibition and his notes stated that "the tower, from the softness of the stone, is supposed to be unsafe and has been bound with iron," so proving Greenway was finally right. However, the tower stood for a further 65 years. When Colonial Architect James Barnet was commissioned to design another lighthouse, he paid Greenway the supreme tribute of erecting an exact, but taller copy of the original, lit by electricity, alongside Greenway's original lighthouse.

Plate 66   THOMAS S. LEWIS. **The merry cricket matches in Hyde Park, view from Park Street,**
Watercolour. Dixson Galleries, Sydney. □ *Hyde Park was named by Macquarie in 1810 and intended
for "the recreation and amusement of inhabitants of Sydney." It was Macquarie's 73rd Regiment who
dug out the tree-stumps to use it as a race-course. The horse-racing crowd attracted illegal betting and
gambling taverns to Elizabeth Street, while circuses, wrestling matches and occasional public hangings
were held in the Park. Eventually Macquarie moved the race-course out to Grose Farm, site of today's
University of Sydney, in an effort to improve the area, and the hangings were confined to Gallows
Hills, now Essex Street at The Rocks.*

*The occasional cricket matches had been held in Hyde Park between the army and the town since
1804. But after the horse racing ended, Australia's fine cricketing traditions evolved here and in the
Domain. From Hyde Park, cricket balls were known to disappear over the low cottages of Elizabeth
Street and end up in the gardens of Castlereagh Street to the rear.*

*Thomas Lewis was an architect and the son of Mortimer Lewis. He may have painted the historic
Hyde Park match of 1843 when Robert Still bowled overarm for the first time in Australia. Lewis was
an amusing character who added humorous and interested details to his painting in much the same way
as Gill. Sheep amble slowly in front of St. James' and the Supreme Court, and a covered pioneer
waggon pulled by bullocks rides along Macquarie Street, passing the Rum Hospital and Hyde Park
Barracks on its way to the bush. The merry lads in the refreshment tent are obviously enjoying the
match. The spectators create a sense of drama with their tight ring around the players.*

Macquarie realised that a larger hospital was essential for his rapidly-expanding town, but that the British Government would never give him sufficient funds to build a replacement for the crumbling old Convict Hospital on George Street North. He therefore agreed to the scheme whereby in return for the building of a new hospital the contractors were given a virtual monopoly of the import of rum for nearly four years. This suited the contractors, Blaxcell, Riley and the Surgeon-in-Charge, D'Arcy Wentworth. They purchased the rum for three shillings and sold it for forty shillings per cask and with these profits all three became very wealthy.

The main hospital building consisted of eight wards on two floors with the toilets and bath houses at the rear, connected to the hospital by a long pathway. The hospital was complete by 1816 and patients were moved in from the dirty and overcrowded old George Street North Hospital. However even in the new Rum Hospital, the nurses were drunken and debauched convicts. Conditions under D'Arcy Wentworth deteriorated fast until they were as bad as before. The convict nurses stole the patients' food and anything else they could find, and the patients in turn stole from each other. The corridors were full of patients suffering with dysentery, so weakened by the disease that they could only crawl to the outside privies on their hands and knees. At night they were locked up in the wards by the nurses and the sick were left totally unattended by the staff, with no access to the outside privies. Since there were no catering facilities, the evening meal was cooked by the patients themselves in the ward, unhygienically surrounded by the reeking buckets that served as toilets at night. Hygiene was virtually non-existent and the kitchen for the staff doubled also as the mortuary.

There was so much sexual activity and even rape of the women patients that it was found necessary to post a Constable on the door of the Female Ward. However he could be bribed with stolen food or rum and was prepared to turn a blind eye to whatever went on in the female patients' beds. The patients sold the daily rations of those who were too ill to eat to the inhabitants of Sydney from the wide verandahs of the Hospital. The doctors in their turn sold the free drugs provided by the Rum Hospital to their private patients and received a large fee.

Female patients were expected to repair their own sheets if they were lucky enough to get any. Treatment was ruthless. Patients were bled, purged or starved until they dropped insensible. There was no operating theatre and the wards resounded with the screams of amputees in the era before the invention of anaesthetics. This version of Dante's inferno lasted for three years under the builder and Medical Superintendent, Dr D'Arcy Wentworth, who was far too busy selling off still more rum to enrich himself to care overmuch about medical treatment or hygiene. Fortunately, in 1819 he was replaced by Dr James Bowman, who reorganised the horrors of the Rum Hospital and it eventually became Sydney's leading general hospital.

Plate 68 FREDERICK C. TERRY. **Bird's Eye View of Sydney Harbour.** *Undated lithograph from the Rex Nan Kivell Collection, National Library.* □ *Possibly Terry went up in a hot-air balloon to draw this magnificent roof-top panorama of Sydney in gold-rush days. Sydney's first balloon flight took place in 1856, a year after Terry arrived from England. The picture gives an enormous amount of information about the changes taking place in the expanding suburbs, at a time when it was fashionable to move out of town into areas like Woolloomoolloo with its then unspoilt Bay or to elegant Potts Point. Woollahra, Darling Point and Rose Bay were still a long carriage drive away, and attracted only the very wealthy who enjoyed the harbour views and the dense bush that surrounded the whole area.*

The centre of Sydney was dominated by the three separate buildings of Macquarie's old Rum Hospital, which by this time had been divided into the home of the Parliament in the northern wing and the Sydney Infirmary in the middle block. By 1885 the first Australian sovereign had been struck at the newly created branch of the Royal Mint in the South Wing of the old Rum Hospital. Beyond the Legislative Assembly or Parliament wing are the twin spires of the prefabricated Iron Church, now the site of the Mitchell Library. The Domain appears vast before the Cahill Expressway literally carved a slice of ground away from it.

The Tank Stream

When the First Fleet landed in 1788 this area was known simply as "The Stream" and its "run of clear water" was the main reason that Governor Phillip decided to move from Botany Bay to Sydney Cove. At that time it was fringed with giant trees, orchids, wattles, vines and ferns but when Garling and Prout painted it in the 1840s these had all been cut down by convicts and soldiers.

The drought of 1788-90 seriously reduced the flow of drinking water in the The Stream and an alarmed Governor Phillip ordered "the stone masons' gang to cut tanks in the rocks as reservoirs." The Eastern Tank lay between Spring and Pitt Streets, while the site of the Western Tanks lay under the foundations of Bond Street, just behind Australia Square. It was these holding tanks which gave their name to the Tank Stream. In his journal, Judge-Advocate David Collins described the Bond Street Tanks as "containing 7,996 gallons of water with a well in the centre over fifteen feet deep."

As Sydney grew, so water pollution became a serious problem demanding drastic punishment and, in October 1795, Governor Hunter ordered that "any free person found using the path to the Stream which supplies the Town of Sydney by opening the fence palings for any purpose, or found keeping hogs in the neighbourhood will be forcibly removed from their home and their house pulled down. If (they are) a prisoner the penalty to be imprisonment and hard labour for the Crown for twelve months."

Surprisingly, the laundering of clothes in the Tank Stream was still allowed, and in April 1803 a Mistress Simpson, laundress, of Pitt's Row (now Pitt Street) was still advertising her services in the *Sydney Gazette* to "the Masters and Officers of Vessels in port that their linen may be washed by her with diligence in The Stream on most reasonable terms". The Tank Stream was Sydney's main water supply until engineer John Busby built his bore from the Lachlan Swamps, located in Centennial Park, and drinking water was then piped through to a stand-pipe in Hyde Park from where it was delivered by horse and cart to each house for twopence per bucket.

By 1835 the Tank Stream was so polluted by the dirty laundry and

Plate 69
*FREDERICK GARLING. **The Tank Stream, 1842.** Watercolour. Mitchell Library, Sydney (ZML 420).* □ *The house on the extreme right, beside the bridge that gave Bridge Street its name, formerly belonged to Simeon Lord. In 1804 when it was built Tank Stream House was the finest in Sydney. Lord died in 1840 an immensely rich man, but by 1842 the house was a lodging house for ships' officers, since Sydney's wealthy set had moved further east to Woolloomoolloo and Potts Point.*

Plate 70   J. SKINNER PROUT. **The Tank Stream.**□ *This steel engraving made from an undated watercolour may have been copied from Garling's painting. Prout spent four years in Sydney from 1840. Alternatively, he may have drawn it for sale or exhibition, and it may then have been copied by Garling. Prout obviously had an overseas market in mind, since he made Sydney look like a picturesque Italian village. The footpath that later became Pitt Street is clearly visible, and the view became famous when it was published in London in Edward Carton Booth's "Australia, Illustrated" the coffee-table book of 1874.*

chamber pots of the washerwomen of Pitt's Row that it was described as "the thick and turbid Tank Stream which now forms one of our main sewers." However, it continued as a laundry for the town until the 1860s, when it was enclosed in stone culverts and disappeared forever in a drain running below the foundations of the buildings between Pitt and George Streets. It still runs due north under the G.P.O., Hunter and Bridge Streets and Henrietta Lane. It emerges under Circular Quay where it flows out close to the Ferry Terminal on the extreme western side of the Quay.

On the extreme right of their pictures both Prout and Garling show a large white house at the end of Pitt's Row, the footpath that eventually became Pitt Street, on the corner of Bridge Street and Macquarie Place. This land was granted by Foveaux in 1804 to emancipist Simeon Lord, who built himself this solid stone home and warehouse, from where he became one of Sydney's wealthiest merchants. Generally regarded as a confirmed bachelor, Lord surprised the town when at the age of 44, he married a former convict named Margaret Hyde. She was eighteen years younger than Lord and had been convicted as a child of eight for a trifling offence. They raised a large family in this house, which was demolished in 1908 in order to build a bank.

In the Domain

Plate 71   AUGUSTUS EARLE. **Mrs Macquarie's Seat, Government Domain.** *Lithograph from "Views of New South Wales and Van Diemen's Land," London 1830. Rex Nan Kivell Collection, National Library of Australia.* □ *Augustus Earle made his original drawing of Mrs Macquarie's Chair as it is known, when he visited Sydney between 1825-1827. He chose some of his finest Sydney drawings and had them bound into a volume which was sold in London as the equivalent of today's coffee table gift book. It was designed to show readers in Britain how their friends and relatives were living in the new Colony. This drawing emphasises the loneliness and homesickness some immigrants felt, watching for the great sailing ships to arrive with the mail from home.*

Earle would have known a great deal about loneliness and homesickness from his own experience. He was marooned for eight months on lonely Tristan da Cunha, when his ship, not realising that he was still sketching on shore, sailed away without him. He was forced to wait on this bare rocky island for eight months until another vessel bound for Tasmania arrived and took him on board.

In his handsome presentation book, Earle described how the route to Mrs Macquarie's Chair was "the daily resort of all the fashionable of Sydney". In this view a perfect Regency buck, complete with quizzing glass on a stick, is seated against the great stone chair. He is dressed in the height of Regency fashion for 1826, an Antipodean Beau Brummell at Farm Cove. Earle described how Mrs Macquarie herself laid out the route around the Government Domain "a romantic and circuitous path of some miles in extent, which ends at the massive rock cut out into a seat and named after her." Probably Macquarie's 'dear, gentle Elizabeth, who never troubled my heart with complaint or tear' was also homesick as she used to stand by the Chair and gaze out to sea at one of the most beautiful views in Australia.

Plate 72 **Picnic at Mrs Macquarie's Chair.** *1855. Unsigned oil. Dixson Galleries.□ Rudyard Kipling once described Victorian Sydney as "a city of picnics and brass bands" and in the perfect summer climate they were a popular form of Victorian entertainment. This unsigned painting has been attributed to several artists including S. T. Gill and Frederick Terry. It is a wonderful scene of Sydney's respectable middle class enjoying themselves on a Sunday afternoon and provides some interesting comments on the early social scene in Australia. Even in 1855 the women and children sat together and discussed their homes, while the men gathered around the refreshment tents, probably talking about the prices of either gold or wool.*

Many visitors commented on these two topics dominating the conversation. "Most gentlemen have their whole souls so felted up with wool, fleeces, flocks and stocks that I have often sat through a party without hearing a syllable on any other subject" commented Mrs Meredith.

Plate 73 CONRAD MARTENS. **Bridge Street in 1839.** *Watercolour from the Dixson Galleries, signed and dated.□ The view is painted from a point close to the corner of Bridge and Pitt Streets looking towards Bent Street and the Lands Department. Washerwomen are laundering clothes in the old Tank Stream while several dejected Aboriginals and their dog sleep by the remains of the old bridge which gave the street its name.*

Bridge Street

Bridge Street derived its name from the first bridge over the Tank Stream, near the head of the triangle of mudflats which formed its estuary, (as shown by the map on the rear end-papers).

The first bridge ever built in Australia was a rough affair of large logs, hastily rolled into place by convicts in 1788 and it soon collapsed, leaving the developing town once more divided into two by the Tank Stream. In June 1803 *The Sydney Gazette* reported that stonemasons and labourers were working on the foundations of a new bridge which "will add greatly to the appearance of Sydney." The following month, Governor King in full dress uniform laid the cornerstone of the stone-built bridge. It took six months to build and cost the government virtually nothing since King, by an imaginative master-stroke, made it compulsory for all inhabitants of Sydney to help with the work of construction, either with goods or provisional labour. In February 1804 the *Gazette* announced "The Stonework on the New Bridge is nearly finished, and it is now only delayed by want of the necessary assistance in filling up the ends. An Order has been issued to summon the attendance of all those who have not hitherto contributed to its completion. The filling is all that is required for its becoming passable for Carts and Carriages. Were the Proprietors of all such vehicles who may reap lasting advantage from it to contribute the use of their Cattle and Carts, they would be amply compensated in an immediate and excellent passage over.

But if the work should be left to . . . the labour of few feeble women, (there) will be a portion of inconvenience that must continue to be severely felt."

It obviously was not left to "a few feeble women" since two months later a carriage drawn by eight bullocks, laden with an immense tree, was the first to cross the Tank Stream by the new bridge.

The infamous pillory, similar to the one in this engraving, stood near the bridge. It was a place of savage cruelty and men were flogged until their shoulder blades were laid bare, while they were held immobile, tied to the triangle, or in this fiendish device, the pillory. If a sentence was for two or more hundred lashes the surgeon in compulsory attendance had the power to stop the flogging and the unfortunate victim, probably insensible, would be carried to the Rum Hospital. Once he had been cured the punishment would then be continued. The psychological trauma of these delayed punishments must have been nearly as bad as the physical in some cases. The pillory had other grim uses. For example during 1797 records show that the courts sentenced three men to be nailed each by one ear to the pillory for perjury.

At the corner of George and Bridge Street stood the Lumber Yard. These lumber or storage yards were a standard feature of British colonial penal settlements. They were in fact convict work camps and the Bridge Street Lumber Yard contained workshops for blacksmiths, carpenters, wheelwrights, tailors and shoemakers. There was also a tannery where the convicts made their own leather hats and shoes. Nails, locks and bolts, bellows, barrels and simple items of furniture for the Officers' Quarters and the Barracks were also made here. Wearing uniforms marked P.B. for Prisoners' or Hyde Park Barracks or C.B. for Carters Barracks, the convicts worked here from sunrise to sunset. If they failed to fulfil their allotted tasks they were flogged at the pillory, conveniently situated close by.

The Lumber Yard gave Bridge Street an unsavoury reputation. Although it was demolished and sold off for building plots by the time Conrad Martens made his painting of Bridge Street, it took years to lose its convict image and become a sought-after residential area. However in 1845, Bridge Street was extended as far as Macquarie Street, once the Bridge Street Government House was vacated by Governor Gipps and the new parts of Bridge Street ran through the former Government house garden. Today Bridge Street is a prosperous thoroughfare and no trace remains of the Lumber Yard or the terrible pillory.

Plate 74   **The Stocks.** *Unsigned antique copper engraving. Undated. c.1800. Author's collection.*

The Convict Builders of Sydney

Plate 75   *AUGUSTUS EARLE.* **The Jail Gang.** *Lithograph from "Views in New South Wales." London, 1830.*

There are very few paintings of Australian convicts. They had no money to commission their own portraits and were certainly not regarded as suitably picturesque for inclusion in most views of the town. Augustus Earle was Australia's first freelance travel artist, making drawings for his own pleasure, rather than as a paid member of a scientific expedition and he probably felt sympathy for these convicts. He drew their portraits some in uniform, wearing the broad arrow and the letters P.B. for Prisoners or Hyde Park Barracks while the others wear a motley assortment of old clothes. On the left is the bell which woke them at daybreak and summoned them to a muster or roll-call, where they were apportioned the day's duties in their chain or work gangs. Some built roads and buildings, some broke up stones while others fetched timber from areas like Lane Cove, which supplied much of the wood for Sydney's earliest buildings.

Earle shows some of the convicts who worked for the chain gangs. Their leg-irons and chains sometimes weighed as much as five kilos and these heavy irons were used to punish recalcitrant behaviour. On arrival in the colony, the most dangerous convicts were marched off to the Government Forge where they were fitted with leg-irons, while a leather cuff was placed underneath the metal around the ankle to prevent chafing sores from the irons. The convict in the leather hat has a string attached to his chain, to prevent it dragging along the ground while he worked. He is also wearing trousers which buttoned at the side, specially designed so that they could be removed at night over the leg-irons. Each convict was issued with a jacket and waistcoat of coarse wool distinctively coloured in grey and yellow, a woollen cap or leather hats, two shirts, a pair of trousers and a pair of shoes. However several of the men in the picture are barefoot and there were many reports of convicts selling off their uniforms and shoes in order to have enough money to buy alcohol to drown their misery.

The man on the right in a top hat, holding a bunch of keys, was the powerful Convict Superintendent. Under him were the Convict Overseers. These men were not chosen for their good conduct but for their brutality and ability to terrorise the other convicts to maintain discipline. For every two years they performed the duty of overseer, their own sentence was shortened by a year. Each Overseer had a daily quota of work which his work-gang or chain gang had to fulfil or he would lose his own position.

The Spanish artist Fernando Brambilla, who visited Sydney on a scientific expedition in 1793, shows a rather different view of the convicts. He painted them pulling the large carts on which farm produce was brought to Sydney from the more fertile soil of Parramatta. He made two superb paintings of early Sydney which today hang in the Naval Museum in Madrid.

The expedition was led by a Spanish nobleman, Don Alejandro Malaspina. The expedition's artist Brambilla, carefully drew many of the plants and flowers that he found in Sydney. Malaspina set up a small observatory at Bennelong Point to observe the southern skies, using the little hut which Governor Phillip had built there to store his instruments. Although Brambilla shows the convicts tugging at the shafts of the heavy carts, the whole scene with the two well-dressed ladies, who were probably officer's wives, has the feeling of a court masquerade enacted by the courtiers of Marie-Antionette at the Petit Trianon at Versailles. It bears little resemblance to the "team of half-naked convicts yoked and whipped like beasts between the shafts, sweating under the weight of a laden timber carriage, whose wheels were sunk up to the axles in mud," described by Lieutenant J. H. Tuckey when he visited Australia.

Plate 76   FERNANDO BRAMBILLA. Detail from a painting of convicts at Parramatta in the Naval Museum, Madrid.

The Carter Barracks
and the Treadmill

When the railway and Central Station were extended in 1906, one of Sydney's most gruesome landmarks disappeared forever. This was the old Belmore Barracks, which stood on the eastern side of Pitt Street, just between today's Belmore Park and Railway Square. In 1839 James Maclehose wrote that the Belmore or Carters Barracks "were erected in Governor Macquarie's time for the accommodation of the convict carters of food and bricks." In those days all goods had to be hauled into Sydney either by bullock carts or by convicts, yoked to heavy wooden carts. Food from the farms of Parramatta was also brought to Sydney the same way.

However, bullocks and horses were expensive to import, whereas convict labour was cheap and available. In 1829 Governor Darling in his Convict Regulations ordered that "no oxen shall be employed in operations which can be effected by men and carts" and so these heavy wooden carts, to which a team of between eight and twelve convicts were chained and harnessed like animals, continued to be kept overnight at the Carters Barracks, where the men also lodged.

The great stone barracks replaced a collection of small slab huts originally built to accommodate the men who dragged the bricks and tiles that built Old Sydney Town. These bricks were made at the kilns on Brickfield Hill, near Hay Street. At the time of the First Fleet the settlement had "three brick carts, each drawn by twelve men. Seven hundred tiles or 350 bricks were loaded onto each cart and each day every cart had to bring in five loads of bricks or four of tiles." George Street sloped very steeply up to the centre of the town and in the heat of the summer the hauling work must have been back-breaking for the convicts, who were often poorly nourished and unused to hard physical labour.

Brickfield Hill itself, before it was partly levelled by the convict chain gangs, was a quagmire in the rain "not only steep and difficult but actually dangerous" and over a million cubic feet of stones and earth were removed from it by the carters to give the gradual slope of today's road. Life for these 200 convicts at the Carters Barracks must have been grim. They were half-starved, plagued with dysentery and disease and forced to work from sunrise to sundown. If they failed to complete their daily work quota or were accused of insubordination by their Convict Supervisor they could be flogged or sentenced to work on the Barrack's treadmill.

These stone barracks built by Macquarie to face Pitt Street with their fine central pediment and massive stone walls were not intended as a jail. Sydney itself was one vast jail, from which there was no escape. The Carters and the Hyde Park Barracks merely provided overnight accommodation for the convicts constructing Sydney's first roads and public buildings. Dr William Elyard the government Surgeon-in-Residence, was the father of artist Samuel Elyard, and Elyard was kept busy during his last summer there when the first mill had just been built, attending to convicts who collapsed from heat exhaustion, after hours spent stepping it out on the treadmill. This treadmill was built at the Barracks during 1822/1823 under orders from Major Goulbourn, adapted from a design already in use at Brixton Jail. The following year the *Sydney Gazette* proudly recorded that a second and smaller mill was about to come into operation.

These diabolical instruments of punishment consisted of narrow revolving steps geared to a mill for grinding corn. The convicts grasped an overhead rail with both hands and trod the narrow steps as if walking continuously upstairs, often for hours on end. They had to step out briskly or suffer continuous bruising on their shins by the next tread as it came round. And so they plodded on, from "sunrise to sunset" allowed "only one hour for dinner but permitted by the Convict Superintendent to descend occasionally from the wheel to repose briefly from their fatiguing operations."

A Committee on Treadmill Labour was appointed by Governor Brisbane to investigate complaints of brutality and to compare its efficiency with the use of windmills to grind the corn necessary for Sydney's survival. In December 1829 the Committee reported that "each of the wheels of the greater Mill, being 18 foot in circumference performs a revolution twice a minute. Each man works on the wheel until it performs 72 revolutions and he has stepped over 1,344 feet. Thirty-six men are employed on the Great Mill at one time and the number of hours on the wheel is greater in summer than in winter." They reported that the convicts trod the equivalent of some 25 miles in a day in winter and 28 miles in summer "in perpendicular ascent". They concluded that "if labour and restraint are calculated to reform or deter from crime, no system of discipline can be better than that of labour on the Treadmill, which admits being regulated and enforced with more strictness and exactitude than any other."

Strictness and exactitude at the Carters Barracks treadmill meant the presence of a brutal Convict Overseer, able to sentence reluctant workers to fifty lashes and backed up by an armed guard. The report concluded that the Carters Barracks treadmill was so successful that treadmills should be introduced in all jails in New South Wales "to contribute to the convicts' reformation and prevent gambling and other various habits which want of employment is generally found to produce."

The convicts themselves had a different story to tell. One wrote in his memoirs, "the brutality used on this piece of machinery is beyond the power of a human being to describe. Unfortunate men are continually falling from it apparently in a lifeless state," and some suffered dreadful injuries when their legs became trapped in the machinery.

Eighteen men at a time were used to work the great treadmill while the smaller could take up to ten. Female convicts were sometimes punished on the small mill for offences like "drunkenness or absence without leave from assigned service." Since the convicts who suffered so cruelly were able to grind half a ton of flour per day on each mill, the report ended on a note of congratulation. "These treadmills are a credit to the indefatigable zeal of Major Goulburn, who spares no exertion to promote the general welfare of the Colony,". In 1841 transportation ended and in June 1846 the Carters Barracks was closed down for convicts and the treadmills removed to enliven the leisure hours of the unfortunate inmates of Darlinghurst Jail. The Carters Barracks became a debtor's prison and later was used as the Belmore Mounted Police Barracks.

Today the Carters Barracks and its treadmills, with their legacy of blood, toil, tears and sweat, have vanished without trace under the platforms of Central Station, but perhaps a small inscription should be placed along the slope of George Street, in memory of the unfortunate and unwilling builders and carters of early Sydney.

Plate 79 GEORGE EDWARD PEACOCK. **Lyons Terrace, Liverpool Street, Hyde Park, 1844.** *Oil on copper. National Library of Australia.* □ *This charming painting may have been commissioned by Sam Lyons or one of his important tenants in the Colonial service. It shows the servant girls with their long shawls walking down to the park, possibly to meet some of the soldiers seen in the picture. The wealthy drive past in elegant four-wheeled phaetons with a uniformed coachman in charge of the horses.*

Lyons Terrace, Liverpool Street

This painting of Lyons Terrace on the southern side of Liverpool Street is the link between two of Sydney's most interesting convicts, whose lives may have crossed briefly but whose destinies were remarkably different.

George Peacock, the convict artist, was a well-educated young attorney from a highly respected family who ran up debts and resolved the problem by using his power-of-attorney to falsify documents for the transfer of stock on his marriage settlement. He married a beautiful but extravagant girl who probably originally caused these debts. She followed him to Sydney but soon left him for another man, refusing to live in poverty in the small slab cottage near the South Head Signal Station which Peacock had built for himself. Peacock's painting may have been commissioned by the developer of the row of elegant terrace houses, Sam Lyons, but he was unlikely to have paid Peacock very well for it. With the current interest in collecting early colonial art, Peacock's paintings today command sums which would have enabled him to rent an elegant home and satisfy his wife's social ambitions.

Sam Lyons came from a very different background. A smart young Jewish lad apprenticed to a tailor, he received a life sentence and arrived in Sydney in 1815. He came from the tough world of London's Dickensian East End and was probably accustomed to living on his wits from an early age. He was extremely intelligent although poorly-educated. He detested the harsh discipline of the Hyde Park Barracks and the work-gangs and managed to stow away on a ship leaving Sydney. He was detected at the next port and returned in chains to the Barracks where he was severely flogged and sent to a Hobart chain gang as a punishment. Showing the drive and initiative which later was to make him rich and successful Lyons escaped from Hobart on another ship. He was recaptured and sentenced to 200 lashes, a punishment sufficient to kill some convicts. He survived the ordeal, and the year his sentence was due for review returned to Sydney and was allowed to open up a small shop in Pitt Street.

He worked unceasingly and, by 1825, had gained his convict pardon and enough capital to set up his home and an auction house in George Street North. He was now married and had three fine sons. To give them the educational opportunities that he had lacked as a child, Sam Lyons worked tirelessly around the clock. He auctioned furniture, goods and chattels and cargoes. His auctions were famous all over Sydney and were held by day, by night and on Sundays. He sold some of Sydney's finest real estate including sub-divided plots at Elizabeth Bay for Alexander Macleay and subdivisions around the Victoria Barracks at Paddington for the Australian Subscription Library.

With the money obtained on commissions he became a property developer himself and drove around Sydney in a showy carriage, drawn by Arab thoroughbreds. In November 1836 he purchased a block facing Hyde Park, comprising the dilapidated home and gardens of the former Sherriff of Sydney with a long frontage to Liverpool Street South. There was a great shortage of suitably impressive homes for rental by important Government officials, who arrived in Sydney with their families, desperate for accommodation at any price. Since the Colonial Government paid a large proportion of their rental, they could afford to rent houses for long periods while awaiting the substantial land grants which accompanied their new positions, so that they could build their own homes. With this rental clientele in mind Sam Lyons built his "fine terrace of six noble houses facing directly on to Hyde Park, with deep verandahs and porticos with balconies above them, halls and staircases of the finest wood, suitable for gentlemen's town homes in the West End of London."

Naturally there was envy and criticism of the ostentatious convict, who was obviously prospering under the system. As late as 1887 Obed West observed that Lyons Terrace "used to have rows of thatched cottages for the soldiers, with neat fenced gardens where they grew peas and beans, where now pardoned men like showy Sam Lyons grow fortunes from their ground rents, with money obtained from drapery, whisky and the commerce of the auction rooms." The *Sydney Herald* under its first owners, Stephens and Stokes, was bitterly opposed to such rapid social and economic advancement of a pardoned convict. They ran articles hinting darkly at shady practices in Sam Lyons' auction rooms.

Their allegations were so damaging that Lyons sued them and recovered substantial damages for libel. A rather hysterical *Herald* retorted, "Sam Lyons, by his own avowal is a pardoned person and produced his convict pardon — everybody in the Court saw it. We can support the existence of a modest, retiring, decent man, who minds his own business, one who wishes only to forget, but we have no forebearance when we behold Sam's bold unblushing impudence."

At the time when Peacock, the sad and unsuccessful convict, made his painting, the area of Hyde Park facing Lyons Terrace was known as Lovers' Walk. The young servant girls, in their long shawls and full skirts as shown by Peacock, gathered there to promenade up and down, hoping to meet a sweetheart among the soldiers who also thronged the area. Frank Fowler described how the servant girls congregated in the Park on their free evenings which was "so thronged with lovers that it was next to impossible for a quiet man untroubled with passion to walk along there".

Sam Lyons continued his extrovert career and became even wealthier. Peacock remained at South Head as Government Meteorologist in charge of forecasting Sydney's weather until 1856 and continued painting. The wife he adored never returned to him and he faded into obscurity but his paintings still are treasured in both private and public collections. Sam Lyons' pride, the row of elegant terrace houses, designed to record his name for posterity, was demolished in 1905, when Liverpool Street was widened to extend College Street into Wentworth Avenue.

Plate 80 **Royal Botanic Gardens.** *Chromolithographic engraving by Gibbs Shallard c.1886 attributed to Frederick Schell.* □ *Sydney's Royal Botanic Gardens are the oldest public gardens in Australia, occupying the site where the first settlers started the colony's Government Farm after their arrival in 1788. It was officially proclaimed as a Botanical Gardens in 1816 when Governor Macquarie built a road through the Domain for his wife's recreational drives to the seat which was carved out for her, and which is still known as Mrs Macquarie's Chair. Gently sloping down to the waters of Farm Cove it occupies one of the most beautiful sites in the world.*

Plate 81   GEORGE FRENCH ANGAS. **The City and Harbour of Sidney from Vaucluse, 1852.**
*Handcoloured lithograph published in London by J. Hogarth. Photograph courtesy Josef Lebovic
Gallery, Paddington.* □ *Angas was not amused when he discovered that his London publishers had
mis-spelt the name of Sydney on his beautiful lithograph of the harbour, when he had sent precise
instructions giving the correct spelling of the title and describing the view, 'The view shows the
approach to Sydney. In the distance are the Blue Mountains, to the right of the City is the entrance to
the Parramatta River, Government House, St. James' Church and the Catholic Cathedral are
prominent, with Garden Island, Pinchgut, Shark Island and Clarke's Island. To the left are the
windmills and jail at Woolloomoolloo with Rose Bay beneath. In the foreground is a group of natives
with banksia, warratah and other native shrubs.''*

*As a a keen naturalist he included some of Sydney's more exotic plants and shows the Aboriginals
living a tribal life on the shores of Vaucluse as late as 1850s. He wrote back to his publishers and
complained about the mis-spelling of the title. Short of money, he asked for his half of the profits, but
received no answer. Exactly a week later news of Australia's first goldfields at Ophir reached Sydney.
Angas was unable to a afford a horse, and set off for the goldfields on foot to earn his fortune. He
proved an unsuccessful digger but returned to Sydney with still more drawings.*

The Hyde Park Barracks

Before Macquarie commissioned Francis Greenway to build a barracks for overnight accommodation for the convicts, they were fed and employed by the Government but left to find their own accommodation. Some built their own small shacks or slab huts, while others slept outside in all weathers. The convicts started to build their barracks in 1817 and it was ready for occupation two years later. It proved to be a handsome piece of architecture, as well as a practical building. It reduced the rate of overnight burglaries, assaults, murders and brawls around the town and provided accommodation for well over a thousand prisoners. They slept in hammocks slung from gigantic wooden stanchions. There were twelve large wards with a night watchman for each ward, whose duty was to call the guard if brawling or sodomy occurred.

To reduce the amount of flogging meted out as a punishment, square towers were built at each corner for solitary confinement of the prisoners. Unfortunately, between 1836-1843 the barracks superintendent was a sadistic Irishman named Timothy Lane, who re-instituted regular floggings for trifling misdemeanours in the barracks courtyard. He insisted that his armchair was placed in the courtyard so that he could watch in comfort as the unfortunate men were flayed to the bone and many were carried insensible to the Rum Hospital by the surgeon in attendance.

When the barracks was completed, Macquarie drew up a list of regulations for running the establishment. He ordered that all convicts were to be searched when leaving the barracks, to prevent them stealing Government property or robbing their fellow prisoners. Any sick convicts were to be employed cleaning the barracks rather than on the work-gangs. The convicts were to work from sunrise to sunset, after which they were locked in the barracks but allowed to walk about and amuse themselves in the Yard until 8.30 p.m. The convict superintendents of the work gangs, who were generally loathed by the other prisoners, slept in separate accommodation from the rest, to avoid the risk of being murdered in the night.

One of the best contemporary pictures of life at the barracks was written by a Mr Cozens, who arrived in Sydney as a convict in 1840.

"We remained on board three days after our arrival; during which period the Superintendent of the prisoners' barracks came on board and examined every man separately and minutely, taking down particulars of our former pursuits, convictions, and places of birth, with our present crime, sentence, and personal description, embracing the smallest scar visible on any part of us. On the fourth day from our arrival, we embarked in a large launch, immediately under the Government House. Here an officer from the barracks was in attendance; and when the complete disembarkation had been effected we were conducted to Hyde Park Barracks. The town being situated at the back of the bay, we did not pass through it, but merely through what is called the 'Domain'. After half-an-hour's walk, dressed in full uniform — grey jacket, white trousers, and woollen caps, with our bag, baggage, and bedding buckled to our backs, we arrived at the barracks, a large and gloomy-looking building, surrounded with a high wall, having strong, folding, entrance doors. Here we were marshalled up in complete battle array, two deep, but in open order, ready for the inspection of His Excellency the Governor.

"In consequence of the 'private assignment' system having at this time been abolished, the numerical strength of the barracks amounted to thirteen hundred, exclusive of the addition we brought. The confused and confounding din of so many voices may well be imagined. The barrack, indeed, at that period certainly contained every evil in human shape — a perfect accumulation of vice and infamy. After partaking of their evening's meal, a large bell suspended in the centre of the yard was rung, and the men were mustered by name into their respective wards, which could scarcely contain them and many 'old lags' were mixed amongst them, which we found to our cost on the following morning, for almost every portable article worth taking was absent. The rations consisted of hominy for breakfast — a thick substance made of maize-meal well boiled in water, which, when cooled, forms a substantial food; one pound of brown bread, and half a pound of animal food. This formed the daily allowance to each person, if I might except the liquor called soup, in which the fresh meat is boiled, with a slight sprinkling of cabbage leaf.

"When mustered in the morning, soon after daylight and breakfast, the prisoners are formed into so many different gangs, varying in number from twenty to two hundred, according to the nature of the employment. Some are sent to the roads, others to the streets, and others to different forts in process of erection. An Overseer is appointed to each gang, who marches his men by twos to their respective scenes of operation and back to the barracks at sunset".

In 1848, as a result of constant complaints from the respectable citizens of Sydney, the remaining convicts were transferred to Cockatoo Island after transportation to Australia had ceased. The next inhabitants of the building changed its gloomy atmosphere. Mrs Caroline Chisholm established a refuge for young female immigrants in the barracks, where hirers could interview the girls under supervision, to prevent the possibility that they would be hired out as virtual prostitutes. Over the following years the building became quarters for Irish orphans, an immigrant hostel, an Institute for Aged Females and in 1887, it was converted to Courts of Law. After many varied uses it is now restored as a unique museum of convict life.

Plate 82

SIR WILLIAM ELLIOT JOHNSON. Old Hyde Park Barracks. *Signed pencil drawing dated 1887.* □ *Macquarie's plaque is still clearly visible but the barracks are now highly respectable Courts of Law. The old retaining walls have been replaced by trees and cast iron railings.*

From the collection of the National Library of Australia.

Plate 83

LYCETT, JOSEPH. The Barracks drawn by a convict. *Unsigned watercolour c. 1820. Fuller Collection, Mitchell Library.* □ *This is the only known view of the Hyde Park Barracks actually drawn by one of its inmates, showing a bleak Macquarie Street and the high walls with punishment cells in each corner.*

The Customs House and Circular Quay

The first Customs duties were collected by Surgeon William Balmain. He was appointed Naval Officer or Collector of Customs by Governor King in October 1800. Since this fund-raising activity was set up illegally by King and was not officially approved by the British Parliament until 1819, there was originally no salary or official building for the Customs collector. Hence the rather ambiguous title of Naval officer, often held by men with absolutely no connection with the Navy, and the arrangement whereby instead of a salary needing the approval of the British Government, they could be rewarded with five percent of the take. This self-motivating system ensured that the Naval Officers would do all in their power to collect the duties at minimum cost to the Colony's sparse funds.

The first Customs duties were set quite high, at one shilling per gallon of spirits and half that amount for wines. They proved a godsend to King, surrounded by a community where nearly everyone drank to excess. With the money raised by Surgeon Balmain, King was able to build a proper jail for convicts reconvicted in Sydney and ensure that the streets of the town were slightly safer at night from robbers and muggers.

Balmain was heavily involved with the other officers in importing and trading in rum and, among brother officers, no one queried his assessment of duties payable, so the system operated to the mutual benefit of all concerned. There was no need for a Customs House for the first Customs or Naval Officers, since this was only part of their duties. They managed with an office and a lock-up in the old Naval and Investment Stores, which were conveniently situated beside the Government Wharf, near today's Loftus Street.

Balmain was replaced by Naval Surgeon John Harris of Ultimo house, after whom Harris Street is named, but he was dismissed by Bligh. In May 1807 Governor Bligh gave the office of Naval Officer to his friend Robert Campbell, who although an experienced shipper and merchant had absolutely no official connections with the Royal Navy. As Superintendent and Collector of Customs, Campbell clashed with John Macarthur over the importation of two pot-stills but underlying this triggering factor was a deeper contention, since Campbell, by his courage, had virtually broken the trading monopoly of the Rum Corps. Campbell's support for Bligh after the Rum Rebellion ensured his dismissal from his official post.

Macquarie, despatched from England to restore the status quo, had no option but to re-instate Campbell as Collector of Customs. However he eventually persuaded Campbell to resign of his own accord, by convincing the honourable merchant that it was wrong for him to assess the duties payable by his great trading rivals like Kable, Lord and Underwood. The Naval Officer's post eventually passed to Captain John Piper, who in 1811 took Macquarie's despatches to England, resigned his Army commission and returned to Sydney to take up the post.

He brought a great sense of style to the Naval Office and, as the port was becoming increasingly busy with trading vessels, was Harbour Master as well as collector of Customs duties. The Naval Office was in Playfair Street, now part of the Argyle Centre. He drove between his mansion at Point Piper, his week-end cottage at Vaucluse and The Rocks in today's equivalent of a Rolls Royce, an imported hand-built carriage pulled by four spirited Arab thoroughbreds, all purchased out of his five percent of the Custom dues. Once again the system suited everyone. Piper, whose portrait by Augustus Earle shows a handsome man with a great domed forehead and fine eyes, charmed everyone in Sydney Town. He entertained lavishly at his home and from her portrait, his wife appeared as a plain and frumpish lady, who also aroused no enemies. Captain Piper in an era of greatly-increasing trade rapidly acquired enormous wealth from his five percent.

Governor Brisbane, who replaced Macquarie, never queried how an impecunious retired Army Captain was able to live like "The Prince of Australia", which was his nickname. But the lovable, and possibly hypermanic, Piper was unable to stop his lavish spending. When Brisbane was replaced in December 1825 by Darling, a martinet for discipline, who was contemptuous of Brisbane's leniency as Governor, he saw Piper's opulent life-style and called for an inspection of the books of the Naval Office. He found that, in spite of the large amount of monies received, there was a deficit of over thirteen thousand pounds, a huge sum in today's terms. Piper had failed to collect some duties and had given his merchant friends far too much credit. Piper was not accused of personal dishonesty but rather of "gross laxity" but the whole system was obviously open to abuse. In 1827 Governor Darling abolished the position of Naval Officer and appointed a full-time public servant on a regular salary as Collector of Customs. The newly-created Customs Department was given rooms in the old George Street Police Office.

Within three years the new Customs Department had expanded so much that they were forced to move back to The Rocks on the corner of Argyle Street. In 1830 an Act was passed creating new Customs positions with the exotic, mediaeval titles of Lockers, Jerquers, Tide Waiters and Landing Waiters. The Lockers were Customs officials responsible for goods unloaded awaiting assessment for duty in the Lock-up Stores. The Jerquers, who sounded more like mediaeval acrobats were in fact Customs Clerks, who checked the papers of incoming ships to ensure that cargoes were correctly described for payment of customs dues. The Tide Waiters lived on board the ship while unloading, constantly tallying its cargo and so preventing smuggling.

Space had to be provided in the ships fo'c'sle for the hammock of the Tide Waiter or a high penalty was demanded by the Customs Department from the ship's Captain. Smuggling and rum running went on

Plate 84   GEORGE EDWARD PEACOCK. **The Custom House and the new Semi-Circular Quay
in 1845.** *Oil. Dixson Galleries.*□ *The Customs House had been built for one year. The picture is
painted from the unfinished eastern edge of the Quay, looking down Alfred Street, named for Prince
Alfred, the first member of the Royal family to visit Australia. Wool bales and casks line the area
where the ferries depart today. The tall-masted clippers await their cargoes; some are stored in a large
lock-up in the middle of the quay while bales and casks lie on the wharf. There is a fence at the Loftus
Street corner and several sentries are on guard at the Quay, to prevent too easy an access of thieves
from The Rocks.*

The Customs House (continued)

continually around The Rocks and Sydney Harbour's isolated bays and to help detect smugglers Landing or Coastal Waiters were also appointed.

To provide office space for so many new staff and their copper-plate ledgers, the new Customs Department rapidly needed more room than they had in George Street. After some years of agitating for larger premises, permission was finally granted from Britain to build a new and purpose-built Customs House, near the site of the old Government Wharf now part of the Quay. Mortimer Lewis, the colonial architect designed a plain Georgian building.

It was described as "over 100 foot long and 30 foot high, with very large windows nearly 10 foot high and five foot wide." The doors were actually eight foot high but in Gill's engraving they look small in proportion to the immense windows. In his *Handbook to Sydney*, published 23 years after the opening of the Customs House, S. T. Leigh wrote, "The Customs House was erected by direction of Governor Sir George Gipps, on the site of the landing of some of the passengers of the First Fleet. In 1844 the Colony underwent one of its severest monetary crises and many were ruined. Many artisans were out of employment and reduced to starvation and so, to protect them, the Governor employed them at low wages to erect the present Customs House which opened on April 1865." These starving stonemasons were so grateful for the pittance they received to feed their families that there were no strikes or demands for higher pay and the Customs House was completed in record time.

Since more staff were being taken on for the new Customs House, the penniless young immigrant Henry Parkes, who had previously worked for five years on a part-time casual basis as Tide Waiter, applied to become a permanent employee of the Customs Office. He was refused although his character report was "without a single complaint." The Collector of Customs who so unjustly turned down the future Premier's application was the authoritarian Lieutenant-Colonel Gibbes, who built Wotonga, now Admiralty House, the Sydney residence of the Governor-General.

Gibbes was replaced by William Duncan, a bookseller from Scotland. He became editor of the *Australian Chronicle* which went bankrupt and Duncan, short of money, accepted a job as Tide Waiter in Brisbane, where he later became the first Collector of Customs, In 1859 he was promoted to Collector of Customs for New South Wales. Parkes, however still harboured a grievance against the whole Customs Office. Nine years later, on receipt of a complaint of insubordination by the Collector of Customs from Colonial Treasurer Geoffrey Eager, Parkes immediately suspended Duncan from duty.

Duncan refused to leave his post at the Customs House and Parkes issued the fateful order for "two intelligent Police Officers to act, if necessary, in enforcing the Colonial Secretary's orders at the Customs House" and literally forced Duncan to stay away from work. Parkes' uncharacteristically high-handed treatment of the mild and scholarly Duncan, generally regarded as a pillar of the church and community, was instrumental in Parkes' resignation after the outcry which followed. The resignation of Parkes resulted in the collapse of the Martin Government. Duncan was eventually reinstated at the Customs Office, where he continued to preside as Collector until 1881, by which time the Customs Office was too small for the work demanded by a busy international port.

Colonial Architect James Barnet was commissioned to extend the Customs House of his predecessor, Mortimer Lewis, by adding an additional wing to each side of the classical Georgian building. To embellish its frontage in accordance with the new Victorian standards of beauty he produced a design for a handsome arcade with twelve polished columns of Moruya granite with an additional upper storey over the existing building.

Unfortunately the survey for the upper storey was not carried out until after the two supporting wings had been built. The belated survey stated that the Customs House was totally unfit to support another storey. There was no way the whole affair could be hushed up. *Sydney Morning Herald* headlines, questions in Parliament, public scandal and red faces all round followed. A Commission of Inquiry severely criticised the Colonial Architect for failing to order an adequate survey *before* starting work on the extensions to the Customs House. However the final decision to proceed in this unusual order eventually turned out to have been made by the Colonial Treasurer. So possibly the tenacious William Duncan won the final round of the battle in his retirement. The cost of demolishing the old Customs House and totally rebuilding the new Customs House was astronomical, and to save money a few of the strongest walls were left standing and incorporated into the new building.

Barnet's handsome new central section was completed in 1887 and was received with general approval by the people of Sydney. The dignified stone portico surmounted by the great stone Royal Coat of Arms looked down in splendour over a semi-circle of the bowsprits of world-famous clipper ships and the Tally Clerks and Jerquers ate their lunches in the shadows of a forest of masts.

At night the Quay presented a wonderful picture. Rows of hansom cabs stood under gas lamps which showed the mysterious outlines of giant sailing ships and ocean steamers with the shadowy masses of the great wool stores behind them. On the west of the Quay the lighted windows of cottages and taverns of The Rocks looked down upon the cove where the first anchor had dropped just one hundred years earlier. But Barnet's alterations failed to give the Customs enough room. A fourth storey was added just before Federation and the present fifth and sixth floors were added in 1917.

The Custom House. Circular Quay.

Plate 85 FREDERICK C. TERRY. **The Custom House.** *Steel engraving dated 1853, incorrectly attributed to 'Fleury' by the publisher.* □ *From the corner of Loftus Street, Terry drew the Customs House with its large windows when Circular Quay was still unfinished. On the right he shows the Macquarie Place Obelisk, which still today boasts "all public roads leading to the interior of the Colony are measured from here". Before the building of Circular Quay, Macquarie Place and George Street North with their deep water anchorages to the rear of the warehouses were the original commercial centre of Sydney. Commissioner Bigge censured Macquarie for building this Obelisk as a copy of the fashionable Egyptian antiquity Cleopatra's Needle which had been dug from a tomb and recreated on the Embankment in London. Bigge considered it a needless extravagance and that an ordinary five shilling milestone would have been sufficient to mark the heart of a convict colony. The Obelisk has survived, a symbol of Macquarie's faith in the future of the city he planned.*

Building Circular Quay

Sadly even those additions to this magnificent building have failed to provide sufficient space for the technology of twentieth century administration. Smuggling of narcotics and pornography has taken over from the old rum runners of Captain Piper's day. The copperplate entries in the ledgers of the Jerquers have been replaced by computer terminals and microfilms, but Barnet's Customs House remains on the Quay, just to the east of the official site commemorating the landing of the First Fleet in 1788.

The whole history of the world-famous Quay is closely linked with that of the Customs House. In 1844 when the Customs House moved from The Rocks there were bitter complaints from the customs agents of the inaccessbility of the new location and that they must "go from the Customs House to the Argyle Street and Rocks Bond Stores and, until the Quay is completed, must trudge through the wearying sands of Macquarie Place or across the Tank Stream."

The reclaiming of the ten acres of tidal mudflats which covered the foreshore north of Bridge Street, the whole of the Lower Pitt and Alfred Streets, part of Loftus Street and part of Albert and Young Streets was the biggest enterprise of foreshore reclamation in the nineteenth century world.

The work was financed by selling off the waterside lands of the old Domain. The construction work occupied many thousands of unwilling an untrained convicts, many of whom laboured in chains and under the lash for seven years from 1837 until 1844. By this time the transportation of convicts had ceased. Even then, Major Barney's great plan was still partly unfinished and construction work continued around Circular Quay for many years. The Tank Stream now lay buried forever under Circular Quay where it still emerges on the extreme western side.

Elyard's painting dated 1873 shows work still in progress quarrying down the great Tarpeian spine of rock from the east side of the Quay. The whole area had to be raised by two feet to avoid the extremes of the tide. To fill in the ten acres of tidal smelly mudflats of the estuary, stones and rubble were brought by barge from the construction of the Fitzroy Dock at Cockatoo Island and from Barney's battery at Fort Dennison. Rubble and giant boulders were also dragged on the old convict hand-carts from the site of the tunnel of the Argyle Cut.

The building of the Semi-Circular Quay was the last and largest construction carried out by the convict population of New South Wales. Precisely because it *was* carried out by convicts, no memorial to their labour exists today. A stone plaque on George Street commemorates George Barney, Commanding Officer of the Royal Engineers and Colonial Engineer.

Fortifications at Middle and South Head, and batteries at Dawes Point and Fort Dennison, the foundations of Government House — the talented and versatile Barney advised on them all. In addition he acted as both architect and builder for Paddington's Victoria Barracks one of Australia's most dignified public buildings. He later became Superintendent of the tragic North Australia Settlement and ended up as a retired Colonel living in Edward Street, North Sydney, close to Conrad Martens.

By 1852 the front door of Sydney had totally changed in shape from the Sydney Cove of the First Fleet. A visitor to the gold-fields named G. B. Earp wrote "Sydney has deep water within a few feet of the shore and wharfs have been constructed alongside which the largest vessels can load or discharge cargo. The Circular Wharf is the most prominent, and Sydney Cove is generally appropriated by foreign merchantment, while the coastal traders have their jetties and wharfs at Darling Harbour. The rise of the tide in Sydney Harbour is now trifling. Nearly a thousand vessels enter the port annually. Ships of all nations put into Sydney to refit and a large fleet of Sydney whalers periodically visits the islands of the Pacific. Steamboats are numerous, some trading between the capital and other ports, while others go to and from the neighbouring colonies."

The name gradually emerged from the Circular Wharf or the Semi-Circular Quay to today's Circular Quay, a misuse of language, for any totally circular quay would have no land base. By 1861 a horse-drawn tram service ran regularly between the Quay and Redfern Station, Steam locomotives on grooved rails replaced the horse-drawn tram service in 1879. Great clippers like the Cutty Sark ceased to lie along the eastern Wharf as they did in the days of Julian Ashton, for by the twentieth century the needs of Sydney's shipping had changed. Major Barney's great half-moon of sea wall was straightened into a rectangle and piers were built for the commuter harbour ferries. The Cahill Expressway now runs overhead past the Customs House, tourists embark hourly on guided tours of Governor Phillip's "finest harbour in the world" and the Quay has entered yet another phase of its changing history.

Plate 86 SAMUEL ELYARD. **Circular Quay East under Construction showing Admiralty House.** *Watercolour, initialled and dated 1873, Dixson Galleries.☐ This view shows the rock face which has now been completely cut back from the approach to the Opera House along Circular Quay. The towers of Fort Macquarie, seen here, have now been replaced by the sails of the Opera House. Comparison between the gigantic rock face and the size of the men carting away rubble shows the enormous task faced by Major Barney's convict labour as they cut this rocky spine away to build Circular Quay East. Admiralty House, Kirribilli, was built by Lt. Col. Gibbes, Collector of Customs. In 1856 when he was Surveyor-General, Colonel George Barney moved in for four years and was able to gaze across the water at the great Quay he had built. Handsome stained glass windows commemorate the twelve Admirals of the Fleet who lived there and it is now the official Sydney residence of the Governor-General.*

Plate 87

JULIAN ROSSI ASHTON. **Circular Quay in 1887.** *Wood engraving from "The Picturesque Atlas" published 1888.* □ *One of Australia's most important nineteenth century artists shows part of Sydney Cove after 100 years of development. Construction work is still in progress using huge pipes which lie beside the Quay. Loading and unloading the great clippers took many weeks using horses and drays. Each heavy bale had to be carried up the narrow gang planks on the stout backs of the wharfies. Open sheds provided some protection from the weather, but the sentry on guard appears to have deserted his post at the sentry-box. The square building to the rear was T. S. Mort's old wool store, now occupied by the glass and steel tower of the A.M.P. Building. These open storage sheds appeared two years later in Charles Conder's magnificent impressionistic oil, "The Departure of the Orient from Circular Quay."*

Julian Ashton's plein-air paintings provided the link between the old topographical style of Sydney paintings and the new techniques and aims of the Sirius Cove Impressionists. Like Martens, Ashton initially came to Sydney on a brief visit, fell in love with the beauty of the harbour, and stayed for the rest of his life. In 1892 he established the famous Julian Ashton Art School which still operates today, and which became a major influence on Australian art.

Plate 88   FREDERICK SCHELL. **Circular Quay West in 1886.** *Wood engraving from ''The Picturesque Atlas''.*

The Sydney Morning Herald and the Gold Rush

When Gill made his drawing showing the newly-built offices of the *Sydney Morning Herald*, the paper was already a Sydney institution but because of its bulletins of the latest finds at the goldfields, it had more than quadrupled its circulation. Today it is Sydney's oldest established newspaper, for the *Herald* first appeared on 18th April, 1831 as a four-page weekly printed on a small hand-press in a George Street basement. It rapidly outsold both Wentworth's *Australian* and the semi-official *Sydney Gazette*. By October 1840 it became a daily publication, but its owner Frederick Stokes had difficulty finding suitable editors. Dismissal followed dismissal with monotonous frequency and in 1841 Stokes sold out to Charles Kemp, his Parliamentary correspondent and John Fairfax, a former English newspaper proprietor. The following year the paper changed its name from the *Herald* to the *Sydney Morning Herald* and by 1853 Kemp had retired and the industrious and ethical John Fairfax had become the sole owner. The *Australian* closed down in 1848 leaving the *Herald* as Sydney's leading daily to break the dramatic news of Hargraves' discovery of gold in the isolated valley of a tributary of the Macquarie River near Bathurst. This area later became famous as the Ophir Goldfields. However a discreet announcement in the historic *Herald* of 2nd May 1851 stated "It is no longer any secret that gold has been found in the earth in several places in the Western country. At present all that is known is that there is gold over a considerable district".

This was probably one of the great journalistic scoops of all time. But, in accordance with his own high principles, John Fairfax followed the Government's policy and at first tried to play down the discovery of gold, for fear it would spark civil strife and mass escapes among a large convict population. Throughout the gold rush frenzy that followed, the *Herald* played an important and responsible role and continually warned its readers of the disastrous social upheaval that could follow as a result of the "curse of the gold-digging mania." None the less, excitement in Sydney mounted as the intrepid and the reckless inhabitants prepared to leave secure jobs and families and go off to the diggings. The *Herald's* circulation increased dramatically with the announcement that "Mr Hargreaves states that from the foot of the Big Hill to a considerable distance below Wellington on the Macquarie is all one vast goldfield and that he has actually discovered the precious metal in numerous places." Based on that statement alone, hundreds of men left Sydney for the diggings, and the *Herald* described "roads alive with newly-made miners, armed with picks, crowbars and shovels or strung round the neck with wash basins and tin pots." Sydney's stores sold out of pick-axes, shovels, ropes, tin dishes, wheel-barrows and flour. On 26th May the *Herald* announced that it had sent as its correspondent to the gold-fields, the explorer Gideon Lang "a gentleman of great intelligence" who would provide further scoops for the *Herald* on "the actual prospects at the gold-fields".

Lang's despatches direct from the diggings were vivid and entertaining and the *Herald's* circulation soared. Every day people crowded eagerly around the bill-boards outside the front door for the latest "Stop Press" news. An editorial described the gold-rush as "one of the most remarkable phenomena in the history of the world, designed by Providence to populate the Australian wilderness." An overseas visitor found that "in front of the office of the *Morning Herald* a large crowd had collected . . . and some drays were already loaded up outside . . . The latest news had been pasted up by the door upon large boards. Each of the mass surged forward arguing about the latest nuggets found" and these bill-boards were still outside by the time Gill made his drawing.

The columns of the *Herald* were now crammed with advertisements for "Waterproof tents for El Dorado", "Superfine biscuits packed in tins", "Red and blue serge shirts and genuine Californian gold diggers' hats", "Real gold-digging gloves" and "Cradles, prospecting pans and galvanised buckets."

The *Herald* ran special weekly Gold Supplements giving practical details such as "the price of provisions are now at most exhorbitant prices. Persons of weakly constitution will be ill-able to endure biting frosts and heavy snows with no comfortable homes and habitations at the mines, where they have nothing but the cold earth for their bed and a tarpaulin to protect them from the inclement weather. Those who are determined to come should provide themselves with warm clothing, waterproof boots reaching to the middle of the thigh, one light cradle, one strong crowbar, one small and one large pick-axe, one shovel, one gardener's trowel for lifting earth, one felling axe, two tin dishes and a tin pot holding two quarts for supplying the cradle with water." The *Herald* warned against the foolishness of "those who have rushed from their homes with only a blanket, a piece of damper and a pick."

Advertisements continued to pour in. The former four-page *Herald* was on some days sixteen pages thick and the circulation figures topped those of all London daily papers except *The Times*. New offices were urgently needed, since the new steam-presses shook the walls of the old George Street building and the number of staff had greatly increased. In June 1856 a triumphant *Herald* moved to this solid stone building on a triangular site, bounded by Pitt Street on the left and Hunter and O'Connell Streets. This was to be its home for the next three-quarters of a century, until 1925, when it moved to its present location.

Offices of the "Sydney M. Herald" N. So Wales

Plate 89   S. T. GILL. **Offices of the Sydney Morning Herald. 1856** *Pencil and wash drawing. Signed and dated. National Library of Australia.* □ *The drawing was made from Hunter Street looking along Pitt Street with its open-air bookstalls and hansom cabs waiting to rush the latest edition out to the suburbs. Passers-by are reading the Herald's pages, which were posted onto these large bill-boards beside the door.*

113

Berry's Bay and Wollstonecraft

Berry's Bay, Wollstonecraft and Crows Nest are named for two unusual men, who contributed a great deal to the prosperity of the North Shore. The moving force behind the development of the Bay was Dr Alexander Berry from Fife, Scotland. After studying medicine at Edinburgh University, he set out on a world voyage of adventure. In the course of service in two of the ships he escaped capture by cannibals and led a rescue party to free the survivors of a Maori massacre on the ship the Boyd. He was shipwrecked, nearly starved to death on a life raft and became a minor merchant trader himself. He sailed around South America's wilder shores, exploring the jungle and risking death on several occasions. After a couple of years, adventure for adventure's sake began to pall. With shrewd Scots acumen he judged that Sydney was the place to make money. In 1807 provisions and spirits commanded incredibly high prices in Sydney Town so Berry purchased a merchant ship. He patriotically renamed her the *City of Edinburgh*, filled her up with provisions and 22,000 gallons of spirits and set off for the Antipodes. Spirits then were bringing a price of fifty shillings a gallon in Sydney, so Alexander Berry was literally sitting on a floating goldmine. Berry became very wealthy as a result of this trading but the *City of Edinburgh* was a leaky and ancient craft, and on the return voyage, she shipped so much water that she sank. Lucky Dr Berry escaped from the wreck and took lifts on a series of other ships, until he arrived in Cadiz. There he met the young Edward Wollstonecraft.

Wollstonecraft was highly intelligent, introspective, obsessional and scrupulously honest. This unlikely pair struck up a friendship and decided to go into business as import and export merchants in Sydney and London with Wollstonecraft, already experienced in the wine trade, providing the London base. Berry accompanied the morose young man to London, met his sister and fell deeply in love. Elizabeth Wollstonecraft, her brother and the young Scots doctor all lived together in London "as one family" while they purchased the ships that were to create the great trading empire of Berry's Bay. Once they arrived in Sydney with their ships Berry returned to London to purchase more cargo, while Wollstonecraft was given a grant of 500 acres of what is now prime North Shore property, consisting of all today's Wollstonecraft and Crows Nest down to Berry's Bay.

Berry used to make the hazardous sea voyages to Britain to purchase goods while the obsessional Wollstonecraft managed the account books. By 1823 they had a flourishing timber cutting and exporting business and had been granted an area the size of a European principality at Shoalhaven. Here teams of convict sawyers felled the timber at the settlement run by Wollstonecraft while Berry organized the shipping out of his Bay. Tobacco was also grown at Shoalhaven by convict labour and shipped overseas in the same way. The bond between Berry and Wollstonecraft was further strengthened in 1827 by the marriage of Alexander Berry and Elizabeth Wollstonecraft. They later built their large home, named Crows Nest House, beside the little cottage of the Crows Nest and gave its name to the entire suburb which later grew up around Berry's house.

As the years went by, Wollstonecraft became more morose and slightly paranoid. He was morbidly jealous of other settlers encroaching near their holdings at Shoalhaven or Crows Nest and even Berry was to claim that, before his death in 1832, Wollstonecraft's "defective temper was to render my existence hardly tolerable." Life must have been hard for poor Elizabeth Berry, torn between her husband and her brother in frequent differences of opinion. Wollstonecraft's moody tempers may have been due to his ill-health, but his financial prowess and obsessional book-keeping provided a profitable partnership, combined with Berry's flair for finding new markets and merchandise.

After Edward Wollstonecraft's death, Berry became one of the few Australian equivalents of the great American nineteenth-century millionaire tycoons. His wealth ensured that he was offered a place on the Legislative Council for New South Wales. He achieved even more notoriety when the fiery and outspoken Dr Dunmore Lang accused him of working his assigned convicts to death in a virtual slave labour camp at Shoalhaven. Lang publicly crucified Berry as the "black incubus" or evil monster of Shoalhaven, but when pressed for a public inquiry was unable to substantiate his claims.

Berry was found to have been, for the age in which he lived, a just enough employer to his convict servants. Lang accused Berry of working his convicts as "Shoalhaven serfs ... in miserable degradation". The preacher continued to repeat these accusations until the Attorney-General laid a case of criminal libel for the Crown versus Dunmore Lang. Lang was found not guilty, although nothing was ever definitely proved against Berry. However, having sworn the Hippocratic oath of a doctor and having tried to be a fair and honest man, the whole affair was deeply upsetting for Berry.

Any cruelty that did take place at Shoalhaven was more likely to have occurred from the deceased Wollstonecraft, in his black rages of depression. He came from an unusual family background. Orphaned while relatively young, he was brought up by his aunt, the writer Mary Wollstonecraft, who achieved her own considerable notoriety as the creator of Dr Frankenstein and his monster, in a series of Gothic horror novels.

After the death of his wife Elizabeth in 1845, and bitterly wounded by all the accusations against him in the Lang case, Berry became a virtual recluse at his great home of Crows Nest House. He let his younger brother David run the Shoalhaven estates, but kept some vestige of control by sending long rambling letters to Shoalhaven by private messenger at regular intervals. One of his frequent complaints concerned the amount of alcohol consumed by his tenants and

Plate 90   *CONRAD MARTENS.* **Darling Harbour from Berry's Bay.** *Signed watercolour.* □ *One of Martens' most exquisite Sydney Harbour watercolours, it may have been painted at the request of his friend Alexander Berry. The picture is produced by permission of Australian Consolidated Press, Sydney, and is part of the exceptionally fine collection of paintings by Martens, which were originally assembled by Sydney bookseller, Kenneth Stewart.*

employees. This was ironic considering that the foundations of his trading empire has been based on his own initial consignment of spirits to Sydney.

The few people who were invited to Crows Nest House were the Rector of St. Leonards, the Rev. W. B. Clarke and Conrad Martens.

Although Martens' view of Berry's Bay is one of his most beautiful Sydney Harbour views in the full romantic and Turnerian tradition, the great wharves which brought Berry's maize, wheat, barley and timber to Sydney are out of sight around the corner of Martens' vantage point. There were also large stone warehouses, similar to these at Campbell's Cove, and nineteenth-century Berry's Bay was one of Sydney's most thriving commercial areas.

Plate 91   CONRAD MARTENS. **Crows Nest House, Crows Nest.** *Signed watercolour. ☐ From the collection of Australian Consolidated Press. After Wollstonecraft's death in December 1832, Alexander Berry and his wife inherited the Crows Nest estate and built this beautiful stone mansion with its harbour view. The great house with its fine stables, library and sweeping lawns was about half a mile from the site of Edward Wollstonecraft's original small cottage named The Crows' Nest. In this house Alexander Berry spent his declining years as one of the richest men in Australia. Sadly, the great house was demolished during the 1930s depression to make room for a North Sydney School situated today between Bay Road and McHatton Street, where the great stone gates of Crows Nest House still front what is now the Pacific Highway.*

Plate 92 SAMUEL T. GILL. **Watson's Bay and North Head from the (old) South Head Road.**
Watercolour c. 1856-1863. Mitchell Library. □ *Surgeon Peter Cunningham recommended a Sunday outing by coach to "The South Head road, along which gigs with well-dressed people and spruce dandies may be seen careering along. Sunday here, as everywhere else, is the great gala day when the various equipages are profusely shown off ... clouds of dust scattering from the carriage wheels of the horses and different groups hurrying backwards and forwards present a very lively picture; an abundance of gigs may be hired in Sydney at fifteen shillings a day so you may readily visit every spot worth seeing. The road terminates at the tall lighthouse perched on the headland forming the southern entrance of the harbour, overlooking the whole southern ocean spread in boundless expanse before you. Midway, a road to the left carries you to the rising ground of the hill named Bellevue, commanding an extensive view of the ocean and all the surrounding wild natural scenery."*

In Gill's time a trip to the bar of the Marine Hotel at Watson's Bay was still a popular Sunday outing and doubtless one that 'S.T.G.' enjoyed.

117

Plate 93   HENRY CURZON ALLPORT. **View of Darling Point from Clark's Island showing Carthona and Lindesay.** *Undated watercolour. Mitchell Library, Sydney.*

Darling Point and Carthona

The promontory separating Double Bay from Rushcutter's Bay ends in the headland which was originally named Mrs Darling's Point. However the name was gradually shortened down to Darling Point, until now it appears to be called after the Governor rather than his wife.

Until 1834 it was impossible to cross the creek at the head of Rushcutter's Bay by carriage and the whole area was extremely isolated. After the bridge was built, Darling Point because of its beautiful harbourside position, gradually became one of Sydney's elite suburbs, full of magnificent stone mansions in the English mediaeval revival style. It was still unsafe at night for many years, and to protect them from bush-rangers and robbers the residents banded together to subsidise a nightwatchman. They provided him with a policeman's rattle made of wood and a lantern, which today seems small protection but at least acted as some kind of warning for the residents.

Undoubtedly the most romantic home right on the shores of Darling Point was, and still is, Carthona. It resembles an English manor house, built of sandstone with a slate roof.

Sir Thomas Mitchell, the famous explorer of Central Australia and Surveyor-General for New South Wales based his design for the house on a home he had seen on England's Lake Windermere. A highly intelligent and gifted man, Thomas Mitchell was not only a fine artist, personally illustrating some of his own books of exploration, but he also carved some of the ornamental stones in the window arches and doors himself. Inside the house, its pointed Gothic windows admit a beautiful soft light from the sea.

On 4th February, 1841, Sir Thomas Mitchell with his wife and nine children returned from abroad and he immersed himself in building at Darling Point. He purchased Lindesay, the charming small manor house on the right of the picture, for his family to live in while Carthona was being built. The Mitchells had twelve children and

Carthona was certainly large enough to accommodate them in suitable style. Sir Thomas Mitchell was a compulsive house builder and improver both in Sydney and the country. He was a man of action and an explorer as well as a man of letters, who translated Portuguese poetry for pleasure. Brilliant, restless, fiery-tempered, he was responsible for opening up much of the interior of Australia. He commissioned several paintings from Conrad Martens and may well have commissioned this painting from Henry Curzon Allport.

Allport, although one of Australia's most highly accomplished nineteenth century artists, seems to have painted rarely. He was extremely well-trained, having studied in England under John Glover. He is supposed to have given the great watercolourist David Cox his first box of paints as well as his first lessons in art when he ran his own art school. Allport arrived in Sydney in 1838 and worked as agent for the Macarthurs at Elizabeth Farm, Parramatta for some years. He subsequently inherited considerable wealth from an English estate and bought a property of his own in the Kissing Point Road area. He also worked for the Australian Agricultural Company during the 1850s and was described on a reference written by Philip Gidley King as a man "of honourable and upright character." He was related to the Allport family whose paintings and books form the nucleus of the famous Allport Library in Hobart.

He seems only to have drawn and painted on commission. His views were generally of important houses, although he did make a most interesting painting of the premises of David Jones in 1842, showing their first small store with a cattle and vegetable market taking place right in front of its George Street doors. This painting of Carthona and Lindesay is undoubtedly Allport's finest Australian work. These two beautiful homes still overlook the harbour today, one owned by a descendant of the Bushell family and the other by the National Trust.

Double Bay and Lindesay

Plate 94

GEORGE FRENCH ANGAS **Self-portrait.** *Lithograph. Mitchell Library.*

GEORGE FRENCH ANGAS. **Double Bay, December 1852. (showing Lindesay at the end of the point).** *Pencil and wash. National Library of Australia.*

Double Bay was originally named Keltie Bay after the navigator of the ship *Sirius* from the First Fleet. However, it is not a true double bay and the picture by George French Angas shows the long sandy spit that only partly divided it in two.

In 1821 Governor Macquarie rode out to Double Bay with some friends. He decided that this was the most beautiful site in Sydney and also possessed better soil than Farm Cove, so the Botanic Gardens should be moved there. He set aside twenty acres there for this purpose but Commissioner Bigge refused to sanction the expense, and the scheme was abandoned.

In 1868 when the Duke of Edinburgh visited Sydney, a special display of boomerang throwing was arranged for him at Double Bay. This was performed by some of the local Aboriginals who were still camped around its shores, where today are some of the exclusive boutiques and European-style cafes in Sydney.

Double Bay has always been associated with the blue of the jacaranda trees. This was due to the gardener at Greenoaks. Michael Guilfoyle was Thomas Mort's gardener, but in 1815 he established his own exotic plant nursery at the corner of Ocean Avenue, where he both imported and grew exotic plants, including many new species of frangipani. One memorial to him is Guilfoyle Avenue, Double Bay, but every jacaranda in Sydney is also a reminder of Michael Guilfoyle. As well as its jacarandas, Double Bay was always known for its palms, staghorn ferns, Norfolk Island pines, and tree ferns.

In 1857, William S. Jevons, as assayer at the Mint, who, for his own amusement, made a detailed study of Sydney, moved out to live in Double Bay. He was interested not only in the incredible natural beauty of the harbourside area but also in aspects of social change in the city and its surroundings. He wrote home in March 1857 saying: "The situation here is most delightful. You must imagine a small circular bay of blue waters, bounded on either side by rocky ridges, either covered by the original bush or ornamented by handsome houses ... On the south side of the bay is a circular white sandy beach rising with a moderate inclination to a few feet above high water, whence a narrow alluvial plain of fertile sandy land extends into the country for about a mile and a half, between the steep and bushy sandstone ridges. Just on the edge of the beach and this alluvial flat our house is built. On our left hand is a pretty little villa in which the old father of Mr Daniel Cooper, the owner of the neighbourhood lives" (later inhabited by the artist Edward Barker Boulton, the cottage stood near the gates of Carthona), "... There is one advantage of Double Bay I was almost forgetting to mention; it is eminently aristocratic, in fact quite the most fashionable neighbourhood."

The house that stood at the end of Darling Point looking across to Double Bay in the George French Angas picture was Lindesay, now owned by the National Trust. It was one of the earliest Gothic homes in the Eastern suburbs and was built by the Colonial Treasurer, a penny-pinching Scot named Campbell Drummond Riddell. Fortunately he relaxed his meanness enough to provide the house with marble fireplaces and cedar interiors, while from the outside it looks rather like a fortified manor house in the Scottish borders.

Treasurer Riddell began his tour of duty in Sydney by writing to the Colonial Office in London with a long list of grievances about his salary, his lack of home leave and about the extra duties he was forced to perform for no extra pay. He continued to pester the Colonial Office with complaints and eventually an infuriated Colonial Secretary in London wrote back the following letter to Riddell at Lindesay.

"My dear Riddell, I am always glad to hear of your progress and wish heartily that you had no grievances to continually complain of, for I cannot remedy them and even to write at length and explain all the reasons why I cannot do so, is more than I can undertake."

For a complex series of reasons Riddell and Governor Bourke fell out and Bourke insisted on either Riddell's removal from the council or the acceptance of his own resignation and it was finally the Governor who was forced to resign.

George French Angas may have gone to Double Bay to visit the Bradley family, who were then living at Lindesay, or he may have been indulging in his passion for collecting and drawing shells. In the same year that he made this painting of Double Bay, he was to apply for the postion of Secretary of the Australian Museum, accompanying his application with a large collection of shells, and his own drawings of shells including some collected at Double Bay.

He was awarded the job of secretary, but it did not turn out exactly as he had hoped. He fought continually with the curator, whose dog was allowed to spend the night in the museum and fouled parts of the building. Angas also had problems with the museum's messenger, who spent his time preparing poultry for market in the basement instead of running errands for the museum secretary. To rub salt in the wounds, Angas was forced to accept a position where the messenger earned more than he did as museum's secretary, due to the messenger's lucrative little poultry side-line. By 1st March 1860 Angas had put in his resignation since the museum had just appointed over his head a director from England, who would be also paid far higher than he was. Angas was hurt at the slights he had suffered, but with a wife and four children to support he was in a difficult situatior. Fortunately his parents and his brother came to his assistance and he returned to Angaston where his father was virtually one of the founding fathers of South Australia.

The Views from Vaucluse

Jacob Janssen was one of the most cosmopolitan and sophisticated artists in early nineteenth-century Sydney. His Vaucluse panorama seems to take its inspiration from the eighteenth-century landscapes that he saw as a young man on the walls of the palaces of the many princes in his native Germany. He left Prussia when relatively young, and worked as a painter in Europe, the United States, Brazil, and the islands of the South Seas before settling down in Sydney.

In Janssen's day the New South Head Road was a rough and rocky dirt track that ran past Woolloomooloo Heights, then the most aristocratic suburb of Sydney, past the rustic settlements of Bellevue Hill, Rose Bay and Vaucluse to Watson's Bay. It was a favourite Sunday outing for horses and carriages to drive to watch the ships as they came through the Heads. Occasionally their passengers would land at Watson's Bay if there was no wind, to save a long day spent tacking to and fro across the harbour to reach Sydney Cove.

Although Vaucluse was regarded as an isolated suburb, the harbour views were so idyllically beautiful that houses were gradually built there by those prepared to endure the rough and rocky South Head Road.

When Acting Governor, Major Grose granted most of Vaucluse to his Quartermaster, Thomas Laycock. It was then known by the prosaic name of Woodmancote. Laycock sold the land to the Irish eccentric, Sir Henry Browne Hayes, Sydney's most aristocratic convict, who as a special privilege for his exalted rank was allowed to live in a small cottage on the site of today's Vaucluse House. As a stout, pock-marked widower of 40, he had abducted by force a young and beautiful heiress. The heiress, a devout Quaker, indignantly refused to consummate the marriage, whereupon Sir Henry threatened to shoot them both. Fortunately he was caught and sentenced to death or immediate transportation to Australia. Alone once more, he turned the overgrown bush around his tiny cottage into a garden full of tree ferns and exotic flowers and encouraged the numerous parrots which inhabited the area. To rid his tropical paradise of snakes, Sir Henry imported 500 tons of genuine Irish peat bog in biscuit barrels, believing that the peat was the reason that there were no snakes in Ireland. Legend tells that Sir Henry would only employ Irish convicts to dig the peat into a six-foot-trench around his property, on St Patrick's Day. Surprisingly, from that day the snakes disappeared. Pardoned by Macquarie,

Sir Henry set sail for Ireland, only to be wrecked on the Falkland Islands for six months before he returned to die in his beloved native land.

For a short time the cottage at Vaucluse was used as a weekend retreat by the wealthy Captain John Piper, then the largest landowner in the Eastern Suburbs. He sold Vaucluse to a young bachelor named William Wentworth. Slowly time, marriage, a mansion, ten children and increasing wealth turned the passionately radical orator and founder of *The Australian* newspaper into a sedate member of the landed gentry. Wentworth eventually became so right-wing that he advocated a scheme setting up a hereditary aristocracy in Australia, rudely referred to by his former emancipist supporters as "The Botany Bay Barons."

By the time that Janssen painted Vaucluse, Wentworth had converted Sir Henry's old cottage into Sydney's first Gothic mansion surrounded by vineyards, orchards and greenhouses. It was hard to imagine that the fiery Wentworth had once barbecued several oxen and provided gin and beer for four thousand people on the heights of Vaucluse. This was to watch his old enemy, the reactionary Governor Darling, sail home defeated to England by night aboard the *Hoogley*. To make absolutely certain that Darling would see his public humiliation, Wentworth illuminated Vaucluse with bonfires and a large sign saying "Down with the Tyrant", since Darling had originally publically insulted Wentworth and placed a tax on his newspaper.

In 1848 Vaucluse House was the first home that the great sailing ships sighted after they came through the Heads. A Scottish nobleman sailing around the world described the shores of rural Vaucluse as his ship came through the Heads "The entrance is through a passage three-quarters of a mile broad, with two lines of rocks rising to a considerable height on either side ... The beauty lies in the numerous inlets or bays which branch off, and when you hear that there are over a thousand miles of shore in the harbour you can judge its immense size. The small bays remind one of Malta, as the water is equally clear and blue. They are very picturesque ... and now and then you see villas nestling among the trees and beautiful gardens running down to the water's edge ... Small boats with their white sails glide around the promontories and form a scene of fairy-like beauty, such as one is only permitted to see once or twice in a life-time."

Plate 95   *JACOB JANSSEN.* ***Vaucluse looking towards the Heads.*** *(part of a panorama of Sydney Harbour.) Oil on canvas. Signed and dated 1848. Mitchell Library.* □ *It shows the New South Head Road as a dirt track with a magnificent view of Watson's Bay and the Heads. Vaucluse House is just below the figure on horseback and, when Janssen painted it Wentworth was still in residence. To the right of the house are quarters for the assigned convict servants, which were probably built around 1829 and demolished early this century when Olola Avenue was created. It has always been considered one of Sydney's most beautiful harbour views.*

The Prince of Point Piper

Due to its superb location, for over a century and a half Point Piper has attracted financial tycoons to build their luxurious waterfront homes here. Racing millionaires, media personalities, Hungarian businessmen, all have made vast fortunes and spent them on mansions at Point Piper.

As far back as the Macquarie period the Point was considered quite the most elegant area for the entertainment of Sydney society. The man after whom it was named was Captain John Piper, who became today's equivalent of a millionaire on the proceeds of five percent of all Sydney's customs revenues. This "farming out" of government revenues for services rendered was not unusual at this time and it was meant to provide an incentive to the collecting of taxes. As easily as he acquired the money, so John Piper spent it. His portrait by Augustus Earle shows a handsome blonde man, once known as "The Prince of Australia" for his lavish entertaining at his harbourside mansion, Henrietta Villa. This domed Regency mansion was considered the most superb residence in the whole colony, when it was finished in 1820. All traces of it have now disappeared and its enormous grounds have been sub-divided, but a few of the original trees planted by Captain Piper still survive in the Point Piper gardens. A true Scot from Ayrshire, Piper had the cross of his native St Andrew proudly emblazoned on the hillside behind his house.

Piper arrived in Sydney in 1792 as a captain in the New South Wales Corps, living at that time on an Army officer's small income. He departed for England in 1811 to take despatches from Macquarie back to London. He realised the potential of the young colony and returned to Sydney to his own expense to take up the position of Naval Officer, which was part harbourmaster and part Collector of Customs. He had previously married Mary Ann Shears, the daughter of a convict, but this appeared to make no difference whatever to the Pipers' social position, once they had become wealthy.

He was known as "a thoroughly good fellow" and his handsome, slightly indolent face was seen at race meetings and all social events. His main hobby was horse breeding and racing and until 1821 he was secretary of the Sydney Jockey Club. He was known as a kind and generous man, who made substantial donations to the poor of Sydney, but his opulent life-style came in for comment and criticism with the arrival of Governor Darling. Darling was amazed and possibly slightly envious of Piper's splendid residence with its elegant "dining room, its banqueting room and drawing room, all furnished in the most tasteful manner" as artist Joseph Lycett described it when commissioned to paint Henrietta Villa. Darling, as Governor of New South Wales, was living in considerably less splendour at his own Bridge Street Government House, described as "a mean and unpretentious building" and "unhealthy as well as inconvenient." It must have been rather galling

for Darling to see a man, once much his junior in the Army, as the free-spending and popular millionaire of the Eastern Suburbs.

Investigations into affairs at the Naval Office revealed Piper's total lack of control. He was found not dishonest, but careless, in collecting the revenues and had given too much credit, possibly because he no longer needed his five percent, having become so rich. He may even have had slightly manic-depressive tendencies, spending while on a series of "highs". The reverse set in when he was forced to resign. Deeply depressed, he asked his personal piper in full Highland dress to accompany his boatman and row him out to sea, as though going out to meet one of the incoming sailing ships that he normally greeted in his official role of harbourmaster. He instructed the piper to play a Highland lament and in the middle of the harbour suddenly, in front of the amazed pair, Piper leaped overboard in a dramatic suicide bid.

Plate 96

JOSEPH LYCETT. **Eliza Point in 1820, the year it was renamed Point Piper by Governor Macquarie.** *Watercolour from the Mitchell Library.* □ *Piper commissioned three paintings of his house that still exist, as well as portraits of himself and his wife by Augustus Earle. This view of his waterfront mansion by convict artist Joseph Lycett is the most interesting, showing the great cross of St Andrew cut from the virgin bush that originally covered today's elegant suburb.*

Plate 97   AUGUSTUS EARLE. **View of Point Piper.** *Lithograph dated 1830. □ Earle drew the house from the opposite side to Lycett. The artist described it as "the first pleasing object to break suddenly on the sight after entering the port is Point Piper." There are many views of this period showing smoke rising from the Aboriginals' canoes, since they carried firesticks around the harbour with them, to cook their catch of fish. From "Views in New South Wales and Van Diemen's Land".*

However he had totally misjudged their loyalty and regard. They fished him out with a boathook and took him ashore. It was found that since he had been dismissed from his position as Naval Officer, Piper's debts, including the wages of the army of servants that he employed, had mounted up alarmingly. The magnificent villa was sold off to pay his financial liabilities as were his extensive lands which stretched around Rose Bay and Double Bay. Piper retired to obscurity in Bathurst and so the "Prince of Australia" lost his principality.

Elizabeth Bay

As one of the fringe benefits of his position as Colonial Secretary, the Hon. Alexander Macleay was granted 54 acres of dense bush stretching from Potts Point down to the eastern beach of Elizabeth Bay. Macleay had spent his boyhood on the bleak windswept moors of northern Scotland and the lush semi-tropical beauty of Elizabeth Bay inspired him to fulfil his dream of creating a botanists' paradise on his land.

Although never a wealthy man, over the next nine years he financed, designed and supervised the lay-out of Australia's most beautiful private gardens. He spent lavishly to import exotic tropical plants from South America, Africa, China and the West Indies, together with spring flowers and roses from his homeland.

With taste and enthusiasm he created a botanists' dream complete with ornamental pools, picturesque grottoes and winding promenades. The gardens of Elizabeth Bay became famous among botanists all over the world. Visitors flocked to them, and one wrote "Nature and art are combined here to form a most enchanting scene. A fairy residence is all that is required to complete the picture, but Mr Macleay has spent too much money on the grounds to afford any large outlay for the present."

The botanist's dream had become a magnificent obsession with Macleay. To create "the most splendid and costly building in the colony" which would be worthy of his gardens, Macleay borrowed extensively and invested in sheep properties, which were highly profitable in the 1830s. Between 1835-1838 he finally built Elizabeth Bay House to the design of Sydney's most fashionable architect, John Verge. Macleay was now 67 years of age, when most men would be contemplating retirement and a simpler life style, but instead he was to move into an enormous Palladian mansion of white stone, "suitable for the residence of a nobleman." No expense was spared initially to create "quite the finest house in the Colony" complete with a magnificent oval staircase, delicate plasterwork, cedar doors and marble fireplaces. Naturally the library was the largest room in the house, for as well as some 4,000 books, it also housed Macleay's botanical specimens and extensive collections of birds and insects. The books were eventually sold to help pay Macleay's debts.

"Quite the finest house in the Colony" must naturally be painted by the finest artist in Sydney. Macleay accordingly commissioned several paintings by Conrad Martens, who also shared his scientific interests. Martens visited Elizabeth Bay House on many occasions and Macleay must have been interested by Martens' reminiscences of his life aboard the *Beagle* and the research methods employed by Charles Darwin on their voyage. Martens' painting shows the house surrounded by an elegant colonnade which, although designed by Verge, was never built, due to Macleay's rapidly diminishing funds.

Macleay's children were also worried by their father's extravagance. "Although it has enabled my father to exhibit a great deal of taste, I am sorry to see him build so large a house and I do not see where the revenues are to come from" wrote his daughter, Fanny, to her brother, William. Her fears proved correct. Macleay fell out with Governor Bourke and was forced to resign as Colonial Secretary. The loss of his salary was a bitter blow and, to maintain the outward appearances of gracious living without the money to pay a large domestic staff, the Macleay girls were forced to perform some of the back-breaking work of Victorian housemaids themselves. Worn out with housework Fanny wrote to William, "very often I wish myself in a bark hut where ... at least I should not be striving to keep up an appearance of respectability. This is the very worst species of slavery."

In March 1839, William Sharp Macleay returned from a Government position in Havana now richer than his father. Shocked by the domestic situation of his mother and sisters at Elizabeth Bay, he loaned his father considerable sums to tide him first over the drought and later the depression in wool prices. But by 1844 Alexander Macleay was unable to repay his son, his debts were still mounting and even the payments on the house were in arrears. To avoid bankruptcy, Macleay was forced to sub-divide and auction off some of the famous gardens. However, because of the depression, only eight plots sold at auction; but these started the urban development of Elizabeth Bay. William Sharp Macleay decided to settle the sizeable debts his father still owed him by taking possession of the deeds of the house while his parents lived there as his guests.

Personality clashes ensued between father and son and it finally became apparent that they could no longer live together in the same house. After two bitter years, Mr and Mrs Alexander Macleay and their remaining unmarried daughter moved away from the magnificent home they had created, leaving William Sharp, a confirmed bachelor, alone with his own natural history collections, in the great family house with its acres of gardens.

Although Alexander Macleay's original dream had soured, his scientific work was to live on after his death, since both William Sharp Macleay and William John Macleay, who later occupied the house, continued the family tradition by collecting items of natural history. In 1888, the combined collections of all three Macleays were donated to the University of Sydney and became today's Macleay Museum. Later Elizabeth Bay House filled a number of different roles but has been restored to its former magnificence and is now a fascinating historic house museum. Sadly, Macleay's world-famous gardens and their gravelled promenades lie buried forever under the bricks and mortar of Elizabeth Bay.

Plate 98   CONRAD MARTENS. **Elizabeth Bay and Elizabeth Bay House in 1839.** *Watercolour. Felton Bequest. National Gallery of Victoria, Melbourne.*

North Sydney and Conrad Martens

Because of the trade in wool, wheat and whaling, Sydney appeared as a prosperous paradise when the young Conrad Martens sailed through the Heads. He had intended to stay for several months and then continue with his round-the-world voyage, as he had already spent a year as official artist on the *Beagle* with Charles Darwin. He fell in love with the spectacular beauty of Sydney Harbour and its magnificent shores, and with Jane Brackenbury Carter, the daughter of the Registrar-General. He married her and stayed in Sydney for the rest of his life.

The wealthy and the famous commissioned Martens to paint the splendour of their new homes. For a time it must have seemed that financial success was within his grasp. His wife owned five acres of bush occupying today's Riley and Edward Streets, North Sydney, and they decided to build a spacious family home there with a studio for Martens. The land had a wonderful view of Sydney Harbour and gave Martens fresh inspiration for his luminous paintings of sky and sea. Possibly Martens' decision to move to the isolated North Shore was influenced by the fact that in 1838, the year that Rebecca was born, Surveyor-General Sir Thomas Mitchell announced that St Leonards', as North Sydney was then known, had been selected as the site of a new town. However, due to the erratic timetable of the North Shore ferries and the difficulties of transport over the winding dirt track which eventually became the Pacific Highway, Mitchell's plan was never carried out.

Martens designed and supervised the building of his own home. Both he and Rebecca sketched it on several occasions showing a dignified stone house with long and mullioned windows, surrounded by shrubs and weeping willows. Rockleigh Grange had the charm of an English country vicarage. In the early days of settlement St Leonards' also had the atmosphere of a sprawling but friendly village, "set in the midst of wild and untouched country ... with a few country seats which have taken over the spots that are most picturesque and nearest to town," wrote a French visitor. As in an English village, social life at St Leonards' centered around the squire of the manor and the vicar. The squire was Alexander Berry at elegant Crows Nest House, a most unusual doctor of medicine who had become a multi-millionaire shipping tycoon since his arrival in Australia. He befriended Martens, bought his paintings and, when times were hard, and the elderly Martens needed a more secure income, used his influence and helped him find a job as Assistant Parliamentary Librarian.

The vicar was also a remarkable man to find in an isolated backwater. William Branwhite Clarke was a brilliant geologist, author and secretary of the Australian Museum. He had an international scientific reputation. As early as 1841 he had predicted the existence of the Bathurst goldfields, but had been requested by the Governor not to publish his discoveries for fear of insurrection among the enormous convict population. His keen scientific mind provided Martens with much-needed intellectual stimulation in his isolation at Rockleigh Grange.

Martens was a churchwarden at St Leonard's Church and probably the closest friend of Branwhite Clarke, who imported the latest books from England and was the first person to tell Martens that his former *Beagle* shipmate, Charles Darwin, had finally published his theory of evolution, *The Origin of Species*.

Plate 99

REBECCA MARTENS. **The painting room (or studio) at Rockleigh Grange.** □ *Electricity did not reach the North Shore until the 1870s, and Martens' studio must have been uncomfortable in both summer and winter. In a letter to his brother Henry, Martens wrote, "My painting room is so cold in winter that I have been obliged to retreat to another room".*

Rebecca Martens outlived her sister Elizabeth and eventually inherited Rockleigh Grange on her parents' death. She died unmarried, and the house was sold. Today there is no trace of this little studio which might have been preserved as a memorial to one of Australia's most important artists.

From Album of Sketches of St Leonards, *Dixson Library.*

Plate 100
CONRAD MARTENS. **Portrait of Rebecca Martens at Rockleigh Grange.** Private Collection.

Plate 101
CONRAD MARTENS. **The West Front from the painting room at Rockleigh Grange.** Dixson Galleries.
☐ This pencil drawing shows the stone walls, long mullioned windows and decorated gables of the home that Martens designed. The house stood near the corner of today's Riley and Edward Streets.

Martens lived at Rockleigh Grange until his death in 1878, surrounded by his extensive library, his musical instruments and his telescope. He painted his luminous and haunting views of the Sydney shoreline and the mansions of the wealthy from a tiny garden studio, unheated and cold in winter, and hot in summer. Lit by oil lamps, it bore a resemblance to a tool shed rather than the workplace of Australia's finest topographical artist of the nineteenth century.

Today no trace of the original Rockleigh Grange remains. It was replaced by a much grander home, which is now part of the Catholic Teachers' College. A simple plaque beside the gate commemorates the visit of the Pope in 1970, when the house was the official residence of the Apostolic Delegate, who later moved to Canberra with ambassadorial status. The plaque states also that the original house was the home of Conrad Martens. Sadly Martens' magnificent harbour view has now been built out, so no truly fitting Sydney memorial remains, other than his own paintings of Sydney Harbour, to the man who created so much beauty.

The Paddocks of Paddington

Plate 102 THOMAS TYRWHITT BALCOMBE. **The Paddington Omnibus.** *Signed ink and wash drawing, dated 1857. Dixson Galleries.□ For a struggling artist like Thomas Balcombe, the only public transport to his Paddington home was by horse bus over the pot-holes and dirt of the South Head Road. The Sydney Echo lamented that "the rack was humane compared to the omnibus of the 1850s. They had narrow boards six inches wide for seats. The difficulty of maintaining a position on such seats . . . over stones, roots or stumps may be better imagined than described." Sydney and Paddington shops made considerable profit selling lotions and potions to heal the bruises on the tender portions of the passengers' anatomy. The drivers were regarded as a wild and drunken lot, who raced each other for money and had been known to deposit their passengers upside-down underneath the heavy coach when they swerved at a tight corner.*

Balcombe grew up on the remote island of St. Helena, where his father was Manager for the East India Company and the family were the official hosts to the exiled Napoleon, before his own home was built. As a child, Thomas played games with the former Emperor. In 1824, when Thomas was 15, his father was appointed Colonial Treasurer of New South Wales, which was surprising since he was a remarkably poor financier and speculator.

Five years later Sir William Balcombe died, in debt, leaving his widow penniless with four children to educate. Young Thomas was forced to take a draftsman's job when he longed to become a portrait artist. In desperation he joined the rush to the gold-fields but failed to strike gold, returned to Paddington and illustrated a book of his adventures on the diggings. His eldest daughter died and this increased the manic-depression episodes and blinding migraines from which he suffered after a bad fall from a horse while on a survey. Embittered by the lack of recognition for his paintings and sculpture, he shot himself through the head in his Paddington home, named Napoleon Cottage after his childhood playmate.

Plate 103 GEORGE ROBERTS, **Paddington in 1863 from the site of St. Vincent's Hospital, showing the Victoria Barracks, Cobbler's Bush (now Glenview and Liverpool Streets) and Barcom Glen.** *Signed watercolour. Mitchell Library.*□ *It is unfortunate for Paddington's fine antique print galleries that there are no engraved drawings of early Paddington. However in 1861 George Roberts advertised his services as a professional artist in Sands' Directory along with Conrad Martens and S. T. Gill. He gave his address as Victoria Street, behind today's St. Vincent's Hospital and this watercolour was possibly the view from his home.*

Cows graze on the paddocks that have become the homes of Glenview Street, while the Barracks dominate the old rural village of Paddington around Gipps Street. To the right is the great white shifting sandhill, which delayed the building of the barracks by several years while its flying sand gave the soldiers an eye-inflamation which they named "Paddington pink-eye". The Officers Quarters, completed in 1842 by Major Barney using convict and free labour were spacious and elegant while the soldiers and their families were housed in miserable cramped quarters, about which they complained bitterly "you cannot turn about without skinning your arse."

Oxford Street, then called South Head Road, still runs past the barracks. The soldiers' wives used to set up roadside stalls there to sell preserved plums and home-made pies to the gentry who rode past on their way to Bellevue Hill or Watson's Bay. Around the barracks clustered the first sandstone cottages described by auctioneer Sam Lyons, who sold some of the first blocks of land in Paddington, as "suitable for mechanics and tradesmen likely to derive many advantages from . . . the new Military Barracks." After the George Street Barracks were closed, the military tailors, saddlers and some of the whores moved out to be near their regular customers. Taverns like the Britannia in Shadforth Street and the Greenwood Tree in Brodie Street did a roaring trade near the barrack gates. George Roberts probably never received a commission for his naive watercolours but today they are valuable for their unique information about early Paddington.

*Plates 104 & 105   JOHN WILLIAM HARDWICK. **Panorama of Paddington, 1853.** Signed watercolour.
Mitchell Library.*

In August 1853 John Hardwick, recently arrived from England, stayed with friends in Paddington, which he described as "a delightful neighbourhood with an immense view in both directions," and "one of the most beautiful suburbs of Sydney". In a letter to his mother Hardwick wrote, "This panorama of Paddington has often gladdened my eyes when I returned from a stroll in the surrounding bush" and "I find this one of the most beautiful suburbs of Sydney."

For his mother to see his new life, he drew both sides of Oxford Street, then known as South Head Road. The top of the panorama shows Gordon's Windmill, built in 1829 by Mr Gordon of Gordon Street. Gordon leased the mill to miller, Samuel Beard, who was still

working there at the time of Hardwick's visit, Beard lived in the two-storey house beside the mill. To the right are the Victoria Barracks and, beyond them, is the Paddington Church, while the view over the surrounding bush stretches away without another building in sight to the Blue Mountains.

The lower panorama shows today's busy Oxford Street as a dirt track surrounded by browsing goats. At the far end of Oxford Street is gin-distiller Robert Cooper's Juniper Hall, which stands at the corner of Ormond and Oxford Streets today. To the right of it is the Stamper family home where Hardwick stayed. Juniper Hall dates from 1824, and has always been regarded the oldest dwelling, purpose-built as a home, remaining in Sydney today. However, recent research by Sydney solicitor Michael Reymond shows that Cleveland House may share this honour since it was built by Daniel Cooper during the latter part of the same year.

In spite of their names, the Coopers were not related. Both were ex-convicts who became wealthy tycoons through trading. Robert Cooper was always known as "Big Cooper" to distinguish him from Daniel Cooper, who was nicknamed "Little Cooper." Robert Cooper obviously needed a large home, since by three marriages he had twenty-eight children to house. "A big masculine-looking woman using her authority pretty freely" was Hardwick's impression of the third Mrs Cooper, his neighbour.

The large house with the double verandah on the extreme right belonged to Alfred Fairfax, nephew of John Fairfax. His Georgian villa had seven bedrooms and kitchen, servants' quarters and stables at the rear, and stood between today's George and Elizabeth Streets. Alfred Fairfax made his fortune selling packaged provisions to gold-miners departing for the diggings and his home was typical of the Georgian period.

The Paddington that Hardwick drew had elegant sandstone homes in large gardens and superb harbour views from their upper windows. These large Georgian homes were demolished in order to build the late Victorian terrace housing that has made Paddington world famous today. Hardwick described how "on going to bed I was astonished to hear the breakers against the cliffs in a heavy surf. The next day I walked to the Paddington Mill" (now demolished and under the foundations of Stewart Place) "when I distinctly saw the waves and a lady resident assured me they were always audible when there was a heavy sea." Another letter mentions "my ramble in the Paddington Woods when I endeavoured to track the mountain torrent ... down the descent of rocks which the waterfall had laid bare" (now today's Cascade Street). "I could not reach the Distillery in the valley, the ground being so swampy."

Today it seems strange that before Paddington became a garrison village its economy was based on gin. In 1817, Robert Cooper, James Underwood and a Mr Forbes were given 100 acres of sandhills and swamps stretching from Rushcutter's Bay to Oxford Street; which were considered useless for agriculture, but had a freshwater pool, fed by a cascading waterfall. By this pool, known as Frog's Hollow, they built a Glenmore Distillery. Possibly this was instigated by Robert Cooper, who must have acquired a knowledge of the spirit trade since he had been transported for smuggling large amounts of French brandy into England.

The three partners quarrelled. Underwood bought out the others and claimed that he owned the land on which Juniper Hall stood. Years of litigation followed, but finally a missing document appeared and Robert Cooper's ownership was proved. He named the house Juniper Hall in gratitude for the juniper berries which flavoured the gin which made him wealthy.

Plate 106

GEORGE ROBERTS **Glenmore Tannery, (formerly distillery).** *Detail from water-colour, signed and dated 1860. Dixson Library.* □ *Underwood leased the Glenmore Distillery to Henry Fisher, who described himself as a "Distiller and Wine and Spirit and Merchant of George Street and Custom's Buildings." Fisher suffered a severe financial blow in October 1844 when a heavy rainstorm carried away the dam above the distillery and one of the workers was swept away by the torrent.*

George Roberts' watercolour shows the building which by 1860 had become a tannery on land between Sutherland and Hargrave Streets. The gin and later the hides were transported to Sydney on bullock waggons along the track that became Glenmore Road and to the left the bush became Underwood and Gordon Streets. It is ironical that today Robert Cooper's old home, Juniper Hall, lies so close to Underwood Street, since Cooper and Underwood spent the rest of their lives in bitter commercial rivalry.

The First Lady of Annandale

Johnston Street, Annandale, built to be "the finest and widest street in Sydney" and Esther Street, Surry Hills, both commemorate a remarkable convict girl, who rose from convict rags to riches and whose husband George Johnston, achieved immortality as the man who deposed Governor Bligh.

In July 1786, Esther Abrahams, a Jewish millinery apprentice, was sentenced to seven years penal servitude for attempting to steal a piece of lace. She was only fifteen years old but, despite witnesses who testified to her previous good character, there was no reprieve; she was also very pregnant and gave birth to her daughter Rosanna in prison just before the Fleet sailed. She gave the father's surname as Julian and said that he was from a wealthy Spanish family and in later years, she often used the name Esther Julian.

Life on board the *Lady Penrhyn* among some of Britain's most hardened criminals could not have been easy for a young and beautiful girl with her first baby. Six of Esther's fellow prisoners had already committed suicide rather than face the horrors of the dangerous sea voyage, but Esther was to prove herself a girl of spirit and intelligence.

Her long black hair and almond eyes attracted the attention of 23-year-old marine lieutenant, George Johnston, who was in charge of discipline among the convict women. A soldier's son, he had already seen active service against the French in the West Indies, and his portrait shows a tall, handsome young man with piercing blue eyes and blond hair. It was an immediate attraction of physical opposites between the blond young lieutenant and the beautiful raven haired convict lass but the liaison that developed aboard the convict ship was to last them the rest of their lives and survive long periods of separation and loneliness. After a year's service at Norfolk Island and accompanied by their son George and Rosanna Julian, Esther and George returned to Sydney.

Governor Phillip had recommended the recall of the Marines to England but George as the Governor's aide-de-campe decided to stay in Sydney with Esther and his son and accept a commission as captain in the New South Wales Corps. Due to this position he was granted 100 acres of land, which covered most of today's Petersham and Annandale as far as Rev. Richard Johnston's forestland at Glebe. George christened the whole estate *Annandale* after his birthplace near Dumfries, in the sheep-farming Scottish lowlands. Together George and Esther supervised the clearing of the dense scrub using assigned convict labour and built *Annandale*, the handsome home with deep verandahs that appears in Hoyte's picture. An avenue of Norfolk pines brought back as saplings from their period in Norfolk Island lined the wide carriage drive from the Parramatta Road.

As aide-de-campe to Governor Hunter, George was required to reside at Government House for long periods, but Esther ran the Annandale property efficiently in his absence. At one period their separation lasted for two years, since Lieutenant-Governor Paterson, wishing to make an example of an officer for trading in spirits picked on George, who had been trading rum for wages with one of his sergeants. George was despatched aboard ship for England but the trial never took place and he returned to find himself a hero in the 'Rum Corps' who were all deeply involved in trading in the Colony. The title of hero was upheld when, in 1804, George, by now promoted to major, displayed great personal bravery and presence of mind and quelled the rebellion of over 200 of the Irish convicts at Vinegar or Rouse Hill, near Toongabbie, with only Quartermaster Laycock and 26 soldiers as his forces.

During his absence in England, Esther had raised his children and with her sound Jewish business sense had made Annandale one of the finest commercial beef properties in New South Wales. Surrounding the homestead there was now a bakery, a smithy, a slaughterhouse with its own butchery, a general store, vineyards and an orangery.

On 26th January, 1804, George returned to Sydney after spending Christmas at Annandale with Esther and his now numerous family. He was afterwards to claim that he found his friend John Macarthur, Paymaster of the Corps, had been unjustly imprisoned in the George Street jail on Bligh's instructions and that Sydney was "in a state of tumult and apprehension with no man's life or property safe against a tyrannical Governor". George was acting Lieutenant-Governor as Colonel Paterson was on leave and, urged on by Macarthur, his fellow officers and leading citizens with a grudge against Bligh, George was encouraged to re-enact his success at Vinegar Hill and lead the march on Government House to arrest the Governor. He was unable to send word to Annandale, or possibly Esther's shrewd commonsense might have saved him from the ruin of his military career. He was to regret his impulsive and costly decision for the rest of his life.

With the band playing, swords drawn and colours flying, and George leading the way as he had done at Vinegar Hill, the New South Wales Corps marched down George Street, turned into Bridge Street and delivered a letter to Government House, signed "*George Johnston* Acting Lieutenant-Governor and Commander of the Corps." The letter, addressed to Bligh, stated that as senior army officer he was "charged by all the respectable inhabitants of crimes that render you unfit to exercise the Supreme Authority another moment in this Colony and . . . in his Majesty's sacred name to resign your Authority and submit to arrest . . . by the advice of all my officers and every inhabitant in the Town of Sydney." The resulting political scandal of the arrest and dismissal of the Governor has some interesting parallels in this century.

To avoid the risk of arrest and the death penalty for mutiny, after a brief period as Acting-Governor, George sailed for England and a Government enquiry which he hoped would vindicate his action.

However, in June 1811 he was court-martialled, found guilty of "causing a mutiny" and cashiered from the army. This was a bitter blow for a man whose whole life had revolved around the prestige of his military career. In view of his previous fine military record and the considerable expense which he had incurred in going to England voluntarily, the Government agreed to pay his return passage back to Sydney, but he was ordered to live quietly at Annandale and avoid all political involvement. Macquarie was instructed to treat him as "any ordinary settler," but warned to be wary of him. By 1813 George had been away from Annandale for four years, but the property had expanded still further under Esther's skilled management. Using the name Esther Julian she had negotiated large contracts to supply the Government with beef and corn and had received her own substantial land grants.

In Macquarie's Sydney, marriage was now important. Many liaisons between officers and their convict de factos had been solemnised at his insistence. Within a year George and Esther had legalised their relationship and their three sons and four daughters attended the wedding. Together the Johnstons now owned over 2,600 acres stretching from Annandale to Bankstown, as well as properties on the George's River and Lake Illawarra. Annandale House, thanks to Esther's good taste was now one of the showplaces of the colony but after his disastrous experience with Bligh, George wished only to devote himself to his family and the management of his estates. Embittered by the indifference of his former supporters when he arrested Bligh, he wrote "every person that promised to support me with their lives and fortunes has risen up after my downfall and my ruin. I alone am the sufferer, having lost my Army commission and six thousand pounds . . . all for conceding to their requests."

Macquarie soon realised that George posed no threat to his own Governorship and after their marriage George and Esther became frequent visitors to Government House. Their eldest son, George, was appointed to an important Government post, but young George was killed in a riding accident at Camden Park. His parents never fully recovered from the shock of his death and three years later, in January 1823, George died and was buried beside his eldest son in the magnificent Greenway family vault at Annandale.

George's will provided that Esther would administer all the property, but that their youngest son, David, would inherit the George's Hall portion immediately. The will caused a deep rift between Esther and Robert Johnston, her second son, who believed that he should have inherited Annandale rather than his mother. Surprisingly, the following year Esther announced that she planned to mortgage Annandale and return to live in England, the country that had sentenced her to transportation so many years ago. Robert instituted proceedings to declare his mother insane so that he could replace her as sole trustee of the estates. The case was unsuccessful but a deeply troubled Esther finally left Annandale to Robert and went to live on the property at George's Hall, Bankstown, with David, where she survived for another 17 years as a formidable and regal old lady. She had days when she was completely lucid but often her mind wandered and she was back amid the horrors of the chained convicts aboard the *Lady Penrhyn* or riding her favourite thoroughbred across the lush paddocks of beautiful Annandale.

Balmain and T. S. Mort

There are few views of early Balmain, since it was slow to develop as a residential suburb, due to the absence of a regular ferry service. Until 1841, Balmain residents either rowed themselves to Sydney or went by horse and private coach. The first ferry service was operated by a leaky old rust-bucket, named the *Experiment* which ran Sunday picnic outings to the area, but by the end of the decade the paddle-wheelers *Gypsy Queen, Emu* and *William IV* were operating a regular service.

Hardwick's view shows the area before Captain Rowntree and Thomas Sutcliffe Mort changed the rustic charm of Waterview Bay forever. He shows the spacious colonial homes with their fine trees and sloping paddocks which covered the area when only wealthy landowners or the small independent boat builder could afford the luxury of living in Balmain. In 1852, at the same period that Paddington visitor John Hardwick made his drawing, Captain Rowntree purchased his waterfront land from Morgan the chemist. Early Balmain was described as "one of the most charming valleys of the harbour . . . and a paradise of tropical trees and scenery" but within fifteen years the trees were cut down and the paddocks built over.

Rowntree Street, Balmain, commemorates the man whose idea of building a dry dock for the repair and anti-fouling of steam ships brought prosperity to Balmain, though he himself made little money from the idea, since he sold out. From a working-class family, Thomas Rowntree trained as a carpenter aboard the ships that called at his home port of Sunderland, England. His ability and intelligence caused his rapid promotion and eventually he became captain of a merchant steamer. He saved enough money to build his own vessel, the *Lizzie Webber*, which he captained on its voyage out to Australia with an English crew, intending to use her as a coastal trader, but on reaching Australia, the entire crew abandoned ship and went off to the goldfields. No replacements were to be had during the height of the goldrush fever and so Rowntree approached T. S. Mort, the successful auctioneer, to sell his ship, since he had decided that his future lay in a dry dock to repair and service the great ships at Waterview Bay.

Mort's astute business acumen recognised the value of the idea and he decided to go into a joint venture with Rowntree. Mort purchased ten acres of adjoining Balmain land and plans were drawn up to build Mort's Dock, with the major capital and shipping contact to be supplied by Mort. To ensure that the dock was built so rapidly that no one else could steal the idea, Mort had an ingenious idea for harmonious industrial relations with his workers. At the laying of the foundation stone he promised "that every man engaged upon the works who had fulfilled his engagement, would be entitled to a freehold allotment in the vicinity of the dock," The unusual incentive worked wonders and the great dock measuring "640 long, 70 feet wide suitable to dock two ships at the same time" was constructed ahead of schedule and completed in less than a year. Mort imported workers to Balmain, who were often housed in tents while the dock was built. The first steamer, the *S.S. Hunter* was taken into dock in February 1855 but by the following year there was so much competition for official contracts from the government-owned Fitzroy Dock at Cockatoo Island that Rowntree, somewhat disheartened, sold out his share for only a small profit to Mort.

Mort still believed firmly in the Balmain project, invested even more money in a wharf and slipway for engine repair, and purchased additional land, on which he built engineering workshops, an iron foundry and a blacksmith's shop with blazing coal hearths for 50 blacksmiths. Within eighteen years Mort employed over 1,100 men around Balmain in shipbuilding and general engineering works, including the construction of railway carriages and locomotives. The greater number of Australia's coastal steamers and harbour ferries were built at Mort's Bay, as Waterview Bay came to be known.

Balmain. New South Wales. (Waterview Bay)

In 1872, the name of the company was officially changed to the Mort's Dock and Engineering Company with many of the workmen as shareholders. This became the most important industrial establishment in Australia and spread into adjoining Johnston's Bay. For over one hundred years Mort's Dock was the pride of Balmain and the main source of employment for its men. However, during World War II the major ship-building contracts were awarded to Government yards. The company ran into financial difficulties and was liquidated in 1959. The waterfront properties were sold off and Mort's great enterprise was partly replaced by 20 acres of container terminal.

Rowntree remained in the ship-building business, living at Northumberland House, Darling Street, until his death in 1902. He became Mayor of Balmain, and was a popular entrant in the annual Balmain regattas, which he revived and did much to promote.

Mort himself never lived in Balmain, but he did much to increase the value of land in the suburb. As early as 1855 he claimed "I am doubling, trebling, even quadrupling, the value of Balmain's property." He paid his workers well and they were able to afford to build their own wooden gabled cottages, complete with bay windows, or their stone and iron-lace terrace homes, which give Balmain its unique character today. Mort himself had an enormous influence on the whole area, not only as the major employer but also as the main landlord, offering leases on homes at reduced terms to "reliable" workers. He also offered shares in the business to workers and foremen when this was a revolutionary concept. His ideas were progressive, and he was generally acknowledged as an upright and honest self-made man, who achieved his own success through hard work. He did much to foster the spirit of independence and rugged individualism which is still a characteristic of Balmain's older inhabitants today.

The University of Sydney

While Edmund Blacket was supervising the first building of the university, the cynical were calling it "Blacket's Folly," since they were convinced that the new university's funds would run out long before it was completed. Many people believed that paving Sydney's roads or the establishment of a sewage system at The Rocks would be of more practical value than a university.

There was also a strong move from churchmen of several denominations that a religious entrance test should be given to every prospective student, but Wentworth fought long and hard to counteract his proposal. He won, and a clause specifically forbidding the religious examination of prospective candidates was included in the 1850 Act which established the university. So in certain quarters it was promptly christened "The Godless College."

Yet another opponent was Henry Parkes, who denounced the new university as elitist. But it was Parkes' eventual introduction of the state school system which greatly increased the demand for entrance to the new University, since graduate teachers were needed for new state schools. Before the establishment of Australia's first university, young men seeking a degree undertook the hazardous and expensive journey to England by sea and were separated from their families for three or four years.

Australia's first university was built on Crown land known as Parrakeet Hill, Grose Farm, leased by Major Grose of the Rum Corps. Blacket resigned from his official position as colonial architect in order to supervise the construction of his masterpieces, the Great Hall and Main Building, which he designed in the Victorian Gothic Revival style.

Sir Charles Nicholson, a member of the Legislative Assembly, insisted from the start that the university should "impress the youth of the Colony," and several designs were rejected as too modest. Finally, in 1854, Blacket's handsome design was chosen because "it allowed for indefinite expansion without impairment of the original design."

Two years previously twenty-four students had been enrolled using the hall of the old Sydney College, now part of Sydney Grammar School. By 1857 the University of Sydney had moved some classes to its own magnificent buildings, but finance was a problem as always. Initially Sydney University was given a yearly endowment only half that of the University of Melbourne which opened in 1855. For many years the Sydney University was chronically short of funds, professors and water. Initially there were only three professors — one for classics, the second for mathematics and the third for physics and chemistry. There was also only one water pump. Water both for the students' needs and for cleaning was carried about the university buildings in buckets by two doddering old attendants.

Constrained by shortage of funds, the university grew slowly. Wearing their black academic gowns, students rode out to university on horseback, or were driven by carriage to Blacket's magnificent buildings, which, apart from the surrounding bush, could have been part of Oxford or Cambridge. The Great Hall itself, with its magnificent vaulted ceiling, was based on London's Mediaeval Westminster Hall, built by William the Conqueror's son in 1097. The seventy-foot tower of the main building can be seen in Elyard's painting and it gave the students a series of magnificent views over the city or the surrounding bush which eventually became the suburb of Leichhardt.

Glebe was still dense bush when Blacket and his family moved from Darlinghurst to the new home he had designed for them on Glebe Point Road. A faded sepia photograph shows Blacket inspecting construction work on the new university building accompanied by his sister, young and charming in ringlets, poke bonnet and crinoline, while he appears serious, and altogether dark and handsome. Glebe was convenient for Blacket's frequent inspections of work on the new University buildings, but it was then a dangerous area, with muggers and bushrangers nightly infesting the bush-tracks that later became some of its main streets. Since Blacket's office was in the city centre he hired four hefty muscle-men as bodyguards to escort him home from the ferry, along the track that became Ferry Road to Glebe Point. Fortunately for Australian architecture he survived the dangers of Glebe's footpads and, when completed, Edmund Blacket's Great Hall was considered one of Australia's architectural masterpieces. Even the sophisticated English novelist Anthony Trollope was impressed enough to write that "this is the finest chamber in the Colonies and no college at Oxford or Cambridge possesses one so fine . . . I certainly remember none of which the proportions are so good".

Plate 109   SAMUEL ELYARD. **Sydney University, 1865.** *Signed S. E. and dated. Dixson Galleries.* □ *Drawn from the junction of the Parramatta and City Road, it shows the low swampy land, which was eventually turned into sweeping lawns and an ornamental lake. Blacket's Main Building and the steep gable of the Great Hall are clearly visible.*

Cleveland House, Surry Hills

Lord Henry Montagu-Douglas-Scott was the second son of Walter, seventh Duke of Queensberry and fourth Duke of Buccleuch. As a child, Lord Henry suffered from crippling attacks of asthma. At Eton College, he was encouraged to develop his talent for painting by art master, William Evans, who had been a pupil of Peter de Wint, one of the nineteenth century's finest watercolourists. Evans showed Lord Henry de Wint's special techniques, using two or three coloured washes with no preliminary pencil drawing, and Lord Henry used these to make rapid sketches during his visits to the homes of wealthy and famous.

Lord Henry's years of travel were advised by the Duke's physicians who believed that in order to cure his asthma, he should be taken away from Eton and spend the damp chilly English winters in warmer climates. This cure was used as part of his education by his tutor, the Rev. Henry Stobart. Together they embarked on a series of prolonged voyages which today would daunt the fittest of tourists, let alone a fifteen-year-old of delicate constitution. Lord Henry, apart from his asthma, must have been remarkably fit, for scorning the boat they rode on horseback the 500 miles from Sydney to Brisbane. Over a period of fourteen years, they visited Madeira, Egypt, the West Indies, Turkey, Greece, South Africa, the islands of the South Pacific and Australia.

Everywhere they went Henry Stobart kept a diary and he encouraged Lord Henry to draw the homes and scenic attractions of the places they visited to show the Duke and Duchess of Queensberry on his return. Lord Henry's Australian sketches are unique, since they are accompanied by vivid and amusing accounts of places and people visited recorded in Henry Stobart's diary.

In March 1893 the *Sydney Herald* announced the arrival by ship of Lord Henry with his school friend, Lord Schomberg Kerr, son of the Earl of Lothian, and their tutor. Mothers of Sydney's single girls of marriageable age were excited at the arrival of two titled, wealthy and handsome young bachelors. Invitations were showered upon them and they dined out every night during their time in Sydney and a party was given in their honour at Government House. Their days were full also; they made eight visits to Conrad Martens at Rockleigh Grange, which they thought a charming house. They purchased six pencil sketches and eight paintings, and Lord Henry also took painting lessons. Martens recorded these commissions with their prices in his notebook. They also spent a great deal of time with the Mort family at Greenoaks, Darling Point, now Bishopcourt, home of the Archbishop of Sydney. Mort had a large collection of watercolours at Greenoaks, including several by Martens which they much admired. On Sundays they heard the Rev. Horatio Walsh preach at Christ Church St Lawrence, and spent the rest of the day with the Walsh family at Cleveland House.

Stobart's journal for October 3rd reads "in the evening there were a few guests at Cleveland House. There has been a great rage here for table turning and we had had great success on most occasions in the drawing rooms of Sydney."

At the time of Lord Henry's visit, Cleveland House was rented to the charismatic preacher Horatio Walsh. He entertained lavishly there in order to attract funds from Sydney's wealthy to his own poorer parish of Christ Church St. Lawrence. This elegant home was ideal for the musical evenings and intimate supper parties given by "the agreeable and cultured" Walsh. It had been built on land originally known as the Cleveland Paddocks, supposedly named by Macquarie for his friend Major Thomas Cleveland who served under Macquarie both in India and Sydney before returning to England in 1811, where he died. Later owners used the Cleveland Paddocks for market gardens.

Daniel Cooper, the convict who became one of Sydney's wealthiest merchant princes, is believed to have built this house "according to principles laid down by Mr Greenway, the architect" and this would explain the elegance of the entrance, and the superb inner stairway and hall. Cleveland House was built to be one of Sydney's finest homes and show the world how the former convict had redeemed himself and founded a dynasty. However, Cooper probably saw little happiness in his matrimonial home and a Deed of Separation records that in 1829 he gave Cleveland House together with its "coach-house, stables, garden and yards" to his wife, born Hannah Dodd, also a former convict "to reside there for the rest of her natural life" and then to revert to himself or his heirs. After Mrs Cooper's death the house was let to a variety of tenants, one of the last being "the agreeable" Horatio Walsh, a close personal friend and later private chaplain to the Mort family.

Stobart's journal records several visits to Greenoaks and he recounted that "Mr Mort is now an extremely wealthy man. He began as a penniless clerk, fell in love with the daughter of Commissiary-General Laidley and in order to find the means to marry her became an auctioneer . . . working for a long time for fifteen and even eighteen hours a day and establishing the first regular public wool sales in Australia. We have always enjoyed ourselves with Mr and Mrs Mort and he is extremely hospitable. His grounds extend down to Double Bay, and are beautifully laid out with the finest hothouse plants in the Colony." Mort told them how much he loved gardening and how he would garden by candlelight at his first tiny cottage at Double Bay, after a long day's work and of his determination as a penniless young clerk to earn enough to build the "noble mansion" that he now owned overlooking Double Bay.

Their religious convictions did not appear to inhibit either the Morts or the Walshes from partaking in the passion for 'table turning'

Plate 110 LORD HENRY MONTAGU-DOUGLAS-SCOTT. **Cleveland House in 1853.** *Watercolour. Dixson Galleries, Sydney.* □ *Recent evidence reveals this may be Sydney's oldest existing home.*

reproduced by permission of Lord Montagu of Beaulieu.

which was then in vogue in Sydney. This involved placing alphabetically lettered cards around the edge of a round table with an upturned glass in the middle, the lights were lowered and everyone present placed a finger on the glass which was asked a simple question. It then responded by spelling out the answer. After an evening's table turning at Cleveland House, Stobart wrote "We were perfectly successful and whatever the explanation, the fact is very wonderful."

Today Cleveland House is used as offices for the N.S.W. Society of Handicapped Children, who although trying to preserve one of Sydney's finest homes, lack Government funding to maintain the house adequately. White ants have eaten away at the magnificent cedar doorposts under the elegant Georgian fanlight. The organisation's own work is vital and no funds are left over to restore the elegantly-proportioned rooms in the classical Greenway style. Possibly Sydney's earliest existing home, comparable in importance to Juniper Hall, Elizabeth Bay House or Willandra, is gradually being destroyed by white ants and the splendours of Greenway's architecture will be lost forever.

Lord Henry's painting shows that the wide verandah with its elegant Doric columns was originally open, lacking the later lattice-work balustrade which fronts Bedford Street today. Although several of Lord Henry's sketches are held in the Mitchell, National and John Oxley Libraries, the majority of his work is unknown to Australian collectors, since it was designed only to be seen by his family. However, accompanied by Stobart's notes, his water-colours and drawings are a unique record of Sydney in 1853. The young Lords left Sydney on October 4th, 1853 and Stobart wrote "We have spent all our Sundays in Sydney at Cleveland House. It possesses what is more precious that the Colony's gold — warm and hospitable hearts."

Lord Henry continued to travel every winter for a further ten years and by 1861 his health had much improved. When he became the first Baron Montagu of Beaulieu, his tours were necessarily limited by the demands of his position. From the House of Lords he took an active part in the great social issues of the Victorian era, which gave him little time for painting. In 1865 he married Lady Cecily Stuart Wortley and was given the Manor of Beaulieu. This is still today the seat of the present Lord Montagu and home of the famous National Vintage Motor Museum, visited by thousands of Australians, who have probably never realised that Lord Henry was one of Australia's early artists.

Ben Boyd and Neutral Bay

Ben Boyd Road commemorates the home of one of Australia's legendary figures. On 18th July, 1842, cheering crowds swarmed around Sydney Cove, excited by the arrival of the largest and most elegant private yacht ever seen in Australian waters. The *Wanderer* drawn here by Boyd's personal artist, Oswald Brierly, was painted black, which accentuated her size and rakish lines. She was fitted with thirteen guns to protect her from pirates on the long voyage from England and carried a paid crew and princely retinue of relatives, friends and employees, including Brierly. Ben Boyd, the tall, aristocratic Scottish merchant banker and stockbroker aimed to found the equivalent of a small principality in Australia by owning over a million sheep and establishing a maritime trading empire between Australia and the islands of the South Pacific.

Nature had fitted him superbly for the role. Handsome and commanding, Ben Boyd had all the charm, flair and charisma of the psychopath, and investors in London and Australia flocked to participate in his enterprises. Backed by their funds, he set up the Sydney branch of his Royal Bank and his own trading and pastoral company named Boyd and Robinson. Within two years he was one of the most important graziers in Australia.

He persuaded Oswald Brierly to act as his manager for the company's whaling and shipping interests at Twofold Bay by convincing him that several years spent in isolation there would make the penniless young artist into a wealthy man, who could then devote himself entirely to his art.

Brierly, who was only 25 when he arrived, was totally under the spell of his patron and friend, Ben Boyd. At Twofold Bay he supervised the building of roads, homes for the whalers and wharfies, a boiling-down works for sheep, and a lighthouse. At first this rough pioneering life was so different from his original plan to become a naval architect that he found it a challenge. But gradually he became disillusioned and anxious to escape from the isolated community and returned to Sydney whenever possible.

Through Boyd he met the wealthy Oswald Bloxsome, who owned a magnificent mansion at Mosman. Bloxsome, impressed by Brierly's artistic talent, built him a small cottage in his garden, so that he could paint while looking across Mosman Bay. In gratitude Brierly painted the first mural in Australia on the walls of Bloxsome's magnificent home "The Rangers".

Ben Boyd himself lived not far away in his large mansion named Craignathan. Today the foundations of this spacious harbourside colonial house with its enormous cellars dug out of the rock, lie under the workshops of the Customs Department, at the junction of Ben Boyd and Kurraba Roads. There is still a Ben Boyd Lane behind Boyd's old wool-washing tanks and great stone wool store, where his ships would lie alongside to load the wool. While initially Ben Boyd's lavish and opulent life-style at Craignathan inspired confidence, gradually the shareholders became uneasy with the management of their funds. Although they received shareholders' reports describing the vast grazing properties, the 160,000 sheep, extensive whaling and and shipping operations at Twofold Bay and the Neutral Bay wool store, the promised dividends on their investment never materialised. By 1847 the shareholders were so dissatisfied that the London office of the Royal Bank sent out their own accountants to investigate. A scandal erupted when the company was found to be deep in debt and Ben Boyd eventually agreed to resign, on condition that he retained some land at Twofold Bay and possession of the *Wanderer*. Craignathan was sold off to help pay off the company's debts.

On 26th October, 1849, seven years after her arrival, the *Wanderer* and her owner sailed out of the Heads for the last time. But now there were no cheering crowds or salutes of guns from Fort Macquarie. Ben Boyd headed for the Californian goldfields to try his luck as an entrepreneur but was unsuccessful. In 1851, still obsessed by the idea of establishing a South Seas trading empire, Ben Boyd anchored the *Wanderer* in a small bay off the island of Guadalcanal, in the Solomons. He went ashore to shoot game, and was never seen again. Natives attacked the boat a short while later and were beaten off with great difficulty. The crew searched the surrounding shore for several days but all they could find were Boyd's leather belt and some cartridges. Without her owner, the magnificent yacht set sail once more for Australia, but the following month the *Wanderer* was wrecked in a storm off Port Macquarie and sank immediately. It was fortunate for Oswald Brierly that he did not follow Boyd to the Californian goldfields but accompanied Captain Owen Stanley aboard the *Rattlesnake* on a survey of the coasts of Northern Queensland, the Barrier Reef and New Guinea. Also aboard was the naturalist and artist T. S. Huxley. For the young Brierly this voyage was to prove a turning point in his career, similar to Martens' voyage on the *Beagle*. Brierly's paintings always show his deep knowledge of every detail of the rigging and construction of the great sailing ships.

After Owen Stanley's tragic death in Sydney, Brierly was invited by his friend Henry Keppel to join his ship the *Meander* on a survey of the islands of the Pacific. In 1851 Brierly decided to return to England and was offered a free return berth on the *Meander*. At this stage Brierly's prospects appeared poor. His period at Twofold Bay had not made him rich, he was unemployed and needed to re-establish his reputation in London. Fortunately his friendship with Keppel was to make him famous. When the *Meander* reached England, Queen Victoria made an official visit of inspection to the ship. Keppel, who was a close friend of the Royal Family, presented Brierly to the Queen. Over lunch Brierly gave an amusing account of his travels and Victoria, charmed by the cosmopolitan young artist, commissioned several sketches of the Royal

Plate 112   OSWALD BRIERLY. *The Wanderer. Undated steel engraving.*

Plate 113   SAMUEL ELYARD. **Neutral Bay with Craignathan and Ben Boyd's Wool Store**. *1843-1846. Sepia sketch. Dixson Galleries.*

Yacht from him. From this time onwards Brierly enjoyed Royal patronage. The Queen appointed him as official artist to accompany her son, Prince Alfred, the Duke of Edinburgh, on his world cruise from 1867-1868. Brierly re-entered Sydney Heads in triumph for the second time on board the Royal yacht *Galatea* which he made famous in a series of superb paintings. His numerous London exhibitions were always crowded out, he became wealthy and was honoured by a knighthood.

At the end of his long life Queen Victoria gave him an honorary appointment, in charge of some of the world's finest eighteenth century marine paintings, as Curator of Inigo Jones' Painted Hall at Greenwich Palace. He often talked of Mosman, where he first met Stanley and Keppel and his voyage with Ben Boyd on the *Wanderer*, which began his remarkable rise to fame.

Manly and Mosman Bay

In 1842 Henry Gilbert Smith purchased a hundred acres of bush and harbourside land around The Corso at Manly, literally for a song. Although superbly beautiful, it was very isolated by road. "Gentleman" Smith, as he was known, was one of the few people to realise the enormous development potential of the Manly area. Eleven years later, Sydney was growing prosperous due to the gold rush and money was freely available for residential land. "Gentleman" Smith realised that now was the time to sub-divide and sell off his Manly bargain for a good profit.

However, in order to show the area to potential buyers, he found himself faced with setting up a ferry service, both on weekdays and for week-end excursions, to tempt potential buyers. The fame of the beautiful beaches and rocky coves of Manly soon spread around Sydney and the ferries were usually crowded by Sunday excursionists.

On arrival at Manly, potential buyers were presented with a brochure extolling the charms of Manly and explaining that Smith's obejctive was "to give it the character of a marine retreat to become the favourite resort of the Colonies. The distance from Sydney to the beautiful and retired site of Manly Village is no greater than that which is daily travelled on the foggy Thames and Clyde Rivers. But a half hour voyage here is temperate and costs less than a shilling, while Manly is also free from dust and microbes."

By 1858 the area had opened up for residential settlement and, in addition to the normal commuter ferry services, a special late-night ferry was provided for Manly residents returning home after a night out in the city. These regulars gradually formed a club to purchase refreshments for the return journey. Sausages and pies were kept warm near the engine, as were the hot baked potatoes which gave the club its name. To continue the evening's conviviality, a good stock of beer and spirits was also provided for the return journey and The Hot Potato Club flourished for many years.

One of the main attractions of Manly Beach in the early days were Cadman's Baths. These were owned by Elizabeth Cadman, the widow of John Cadman of Cadman's Cottage, now the show-piece of The Rocks. Elizabeth Cadman was a former convict and when her husband died, she moved away from their little cottage by the first ship-yard on George Street North and with great foresight anticipated Manly's popularity. As well as changing accommodation, Cadman's Baths advertised the delights of hot salt water baths for two shillings or bracing cold showers for a shilling.

Mosman was named for its first developer, Archibald Mosman, son of the Deputy Lord Lieutenant of Lanarkshire in Scotland. He came to Australia with some commercial experience, having already made a small fortune growing sugar cane in the West Indies. In 1831 he was given a grant of four acres of land between Sirius Cove and Mosman Bay. He used assigned convict labour to build a 600-foot jetty and a large stone storehouse called The Barn, which is today still used as a meeting place by Mosman's Boy Scouts. Convict labour also helped to build his handsome stone home of The Nest, on today's Badham Avenue. The reason for its name can be seen from Martens' painting of the area, and the wonderful view that it commanded over the water like an eagle's eyrie high above the Bay. To carry out his developments at Mosman, Archibald sold off his George Street warehouse and financed the building of his wharf, warehouses and Mosman home himself. Mosman's original estate eventually extended from the shoreline to today's Military Road below Cremorne and along the Spit Junction down to Raglan Street.

It would have been impossible for Archibald Mosman to have carried out his whaling operations any closer to Sydney, due to the dreadful stench from long-dead whales. This ensured that his whaling business was granted this beautiful land then deemed to be too far away for residential use. The area gradually acquired the name of Mosman's Wharf and later on was to become Mosman's Bay. Whales were the great natural resource of the early nineteenth century. They provided oil for lamps and bones for the tight corsets so necessary for the Victorian lady, and the unfortunate whales were savagely pursued to provide these essentials of early Victorian life. In 1834 Mosman perhaps saw the forthcoming downturn in whaling and sold out his whaling interests and home at Mosman and went off to lead a quiet pastoral life at Glen Innes.

After Mosman had departed, the Bay was used to careen and repair sailing ships, since in the 1840s, incredible though it seems today, the nearest dry dock to Sydney was at Bombay in India. By the late 1840s, there were plans to turn the old careening area, where the ships were laid on their sides and anti-fouled in the shallows, into a dry dock. But T. S. Mort and his dock at Balmain rendered the idea superfluous. This was fortunate for Mosman's scenery, since it would be a sadly different place today had commercial development of this kind been permitted.

At the time when Martens made his watercolour, Archibald Mosman had departed and the wharf area was run by a Mr Stirling, who advertised storage facilities at Mosman Wharf for 3,000 barrels of whale oil.

In 1859 Richard Hayes Harnett purchased Mosman's home and estate with the idea of turning it into a pleasure resort complete with sideshows, attractions and dancing to Crowe's Celebration Quadrille Band. Fortunately for Mosman's quiet shores, this scheme was not a success, as it was still considered too far from the city. Harnett lost money and was forced to sell out. His ferry services had been crowded at the weekends but it was still thought too far from the city to live.

However Harnett still believed in the future of the North Shore as a

Plate 114   *SAMUEL THOMAS GILL.* **The approach to Manly Beach.** *Lithograph, signed and dated 1856. From Gill's book "Scenery in and Around Sydney," held by the Mitchell Library.*

residential area, and above all that beautiful Mosman, must eventually become one of Sydney's finest suburbs. In 1876 he inherited a substantial sum of money and re-purchased his original holdings in Mosman, together with a further 300 acres to put his dream into reality. This time his task was easier, as the bush tracks from the North Shore had been cleared for horse-drawn traffic by the Government establishing fortifications at Middle Harbour, Georges and Bradley's Head against a possible Russian invasion, giving rise to the name Military Road.

This time Harnett's schemes proved successful. He ran his own ferry service from Circular Quay to Archibald Mosman's old jetty, operating now with regular time-tables rather than waiting until the ferry was full enough to start its journey. He also owned a horse-drawn omnibus service that connected up with his own ferries to Mosman Junction. His sub-divisions sold so well that he built a public hall close to the present Post Office. Mosman became Sydney's elegant residential suburb for the landed gentry. Houses resplendent with cupolas, domes, gables, bell-towers, flagpoles and summer pavilions were built, and their leafy gardens with fine harbour views were the ideal settings for garden parties. From the early beginnings of a jetty and Archibald Mosman's smelly whale carcases, the area had been totally transformed in half a century due to the drive, initiative and vision of Richard Hayes Harnett.

Plate 115 CONRAD MARTENS. **Mosman's Bay 1842-1843.** Signed watercolour. □ This is a characteristic Martens with its picturesque tree in the foreground swathed in hanging vines. Martens looks across to Archibald Mosman's former colonial home on Badham Avenue with its flagpost. Below are the stone stores of Mosman's former whaling ventures beside his wharf. A ship can be seen lying on its side for cleaning and repair of its hull, known as careening. For a most important historical painting of Mosman in its earliest days, it deserves to be better known. The picture was purchased by Sir William Dixson, the wealthy collector who used his riches to help build up a visual portrait of the story of Australia, in order to increase the country's sense of pride in its own history. The picture was donated by him to all Australians as part of his important collection of early Australian art, which today is held by the Dixson Galleries, Sydney. But Sir William Dixson was not just a wealthy tobacco heir who donated pictures to the nation. He used his time and his keen intelligence to trace the lives of the artists and the histories of the buildings they painted and greatly enriched Australia's cultural background.

*MOSSMAN'S BAY
(NEAR) SYDNEY*

Plate 116   S. T. GILL. **Detail from a watercolour showing Mosman's Bay about 1860.** *From the collection of the Mitchell Library.* □ *Gill shows Avenue Road leading down to the Mosman wharf. Some of these buildings are still in use today. High on the right, along today's Badham Avenue was the original home of Archibald Mosman, called The Nest, now commemorated by a flag-pole. In 1859 the house was purchased by Richard Hayes Harnett, the Mosman property developer. He tried to turn Mosman's old whaling station into a pleasure resort, complete with two ferries, pigeon shooting, coconut shies, organised walking trips and picnics on Sundays. He built Mosman's first roads, ran a horse bus service and became one of the first directors of the North Shore Ferry Company, which opened up many harbour areas for residential development. On the left is Bloxsome's home, The Rangers, with the tiny cottage where Oswald Brierly used to live and paint.*

147

Plate 117   *JULIAN ROSSI ASHTON* **The Mosman Ferry in 1888.** *Signed and dated watercolour, reproduced by permission of the National Gallery of Victoria and the Directors of the Julian Ashton Art School, Sydney.* □ *Julian Ashton originally emigrated to Melbourne and planned to return to England. A holiday in Sydney changed his plans. He fell in love with its "winding streets and picturesque old buildings" and stayed for the rest of his life. He never tired of painting Sydney Harbour. This is one of his finest watercolours with its changing patterns of reflected light rippling across the water. Ashton revolutionised Australian art by making his entire painting outdoors, rather than using quick pencil sketches as a basis for a studio landscape, as previous artists had done.*

Plate 118   EDWARD BARKER BOULTON. **Port Jackson from the North Shore and City of Sydney.** *Chromolithograph dated 1879.* ☐ *Edward Barker Boulton is believed to have been a pupil of Martens. His skilful handling of colour and shading show that he had some professional training, although he is supposed to have painted entirely for his own pleasure. He is also presumed to be the "E.B.B.", whose album of pencil sketches in the Mitchell Library contains views of Vaucluse, Watson's Bay, Point Piper and Rose Bay in the 1840s when Barker Boulton lived in a cottage in the grounds of Carthona at Darling Point. He arrived in Australia in 1836 and died on his grazing property near Walcha in 1895.*

This superb panorama painted from Kurraba Point in 1879 shows a tranquil and rustic North Shore, where cows still graze on the undeveloped bush between Neutral Bay and Kirribilli. The artist looks across to his old home at Darling Point over Garden Island and the tranquil waters of Port Jackson. On the extreme left is Cremorne, with the inlet of Shell Cove and the headland of Kurraba Point adjoining Neutral Bay and Careening Cove. A clipper in full sail passes Kirribilli. On the right is Milson's Point, with Sydney directly facing it across the water, while ships lie at anchor in front of the Domain. This rich use of colour is typical of the late Victorian period and shows the high standard of colour printing then obtainable through chromolithography.

Photograph by Tony Carpenter and picture reproduced by courtesy of the Josef Lebovic Gallery, Sydney.

149

Plate 119   S. T. GILL. *View . . . from the North Shore, 1861.* Watercolour. Dixson Galleries (ZDG 187). □
*Gill's watercolour was painted five years after his detailed lithograph of Milson's Point on the facing
page, drawn to illustrate his book, "Scenery in and around Sydney." This watercolour highlights the
difficulties experienced by the pioneer settlers of North Shore. In 1861 most of the trees on the lower
slopes of North Sydney and St. Leonards had been cut down by the timber-getters, who lived isolated
lonely lives in these tiny slab huts, which were virtually unchanged from those built by the men of the
First Fleet. These timber-getters of the North Shore provided the giant redwoods and cedars used to
build Sydney's elegant Colonial homes and the enormous turpentines needed for the wharves of
Circular Quay.*

*Unlike the lush shores of the Eastern suburbs at this period, here are no elegant carriages or Gothic
harbourside villas. Instead Gill shows that the North Shore consisted of red dust, stony ground and a
rough bullock track bordered by workmen's cottages, which eventually became the Pacific Highway.
Another Gill lithograph of the same area is on the facing page.*

The First Ferries

"THE OLD COMMODORE,"
BILLY BLUE.

Plate 120   S. T. GILL. **Milson's Point, 1856.** *Lithograph.*

*Plate 121   "**The Old Commodore**": Billy Blue.* *Lithograph.*

The first ferryman were ex-convicts like Billy Blue, Macquarie's former water bailiff. In 1830 he went into business running a rowboat ferry service similar to today's water-taxis. This gigantic Jamaican, who by then was in his eighties, persuaded his passengers to pay him for the pleasure of rowing themselves across the harbour in his boat and made them laugh so much that they paid up willingly. His sons carried on his ferry service until 1842, when this large paddle-wheel punt driven by a steam engine, began operating between Dawes Point and Blue's Point. It had no fixed timetable and only took off when the ferryman had a suitable load.

In 1860, the North Shore Ferry Company was founded and the company ran ferries with a regular timetable from Circular Quay. Six years later, by popular demand, a cable tramway started up from Milson's Point Wharf, seen here before the terminal building was constructed, and Ridge Street, North Sydney. (Both lithographs are from the Mitchell Library).

The Sydney Regatta

Plate 122 **The Sydney Anniversary Regatta.** *Attributed to Owen Stanley. Watercolour. Courtesy Christies, London.*

In 1827 the only registered owner of a sailing boat kept purely for pleasure purposes was Robert Campbell, who moored his three-tonner with gunter sails at Campbell's Wharf. But the first regatta held on Sydney waters was to change this and sailing for pleasure gradually became an everyday sight on the Harbour.

Australia's first regatta was organised by the officers of two warships anchored in the harbour, *H.M.S. Success* and *H.M.S. Rainbow*. The first race, for the crews of the warships rowing their longboats, was won by the crew of the *H.M.S. Mercury*. Sir Francis Forbes, the first Chief Justice of the Colony and Lady Forbes, were invited aboard both vessels for drinks and entertainments and Lady Forbes later wrote down her impressions of the day. "The second race was a sailing match for a purse of 50 Spanish dollars, won by Lieutenant Preston's *Black Swan* and the course was from the Flagship in Sydney Cove around the Sow and Pigs Reef and back. The third race was a rowing match, eight boats started and the course was from Dawes' Point, round Pinchgut Island and back. The races were the cause of much excitement and, from the cheering of the people assembled in large numbers at Dawes' Point and Mrs Macquarie's Chair, this win seemed a popular one." The entrants in the third race were the famous Sydney watermen, who plied for hire on their long narrow skiffs on the waters of the harbour. These watermen were highly skilled, as many of them had gained their experience in handling whaleboats on high and dangerous seas. They were used to racing against each other when rowing out to Watson's Bay to meet newly arrived vessels, but this was the first time they had raced or sailed purely for pleasure.

Lady Forbes recounted the start of a true Sydney Regatta tradition with ample liquid refreshment. Other guests on board included Captain Piper of Point Piper, Dr Bland and Dr D'Arcy Wentworth. "The band of the 57th Regiment played dance music. Dancing the French quadrilles kept the young people amused between races and the junior officers joined in with great spirit. The weather was delightful and I shall always look back with an agreeable remembrance to the first Australian Regatta."

This regatta attracted such enormous crowds that by popular demand regattas were held annually in January, but it was not until ten years later in 1837 that it became known as the Anniversary Regatta, to celebrate the foundation of New South Wales. It was subsequently renamed the "Australia Day Regatta" and as such, it is the oldest regularly-organised regatta held anywhere in the world.

The success of these early regattas prompted Sydney sportsmen to acquire private yachts to race in them. Due to the increasing prosperity of Sydney, sailing rapidly became one of the most popular of sports, since the spacious waters of the harbour were ideal for pleasure sailing. This charming small painting entitled "Sydney Anniversary Regatta", recently auctioned by Christies in London, may be the work of a visiting officer aboard one of the ships that anchored in the harbour to watch the regatta.

A Proposal for Bridging
the Harbour

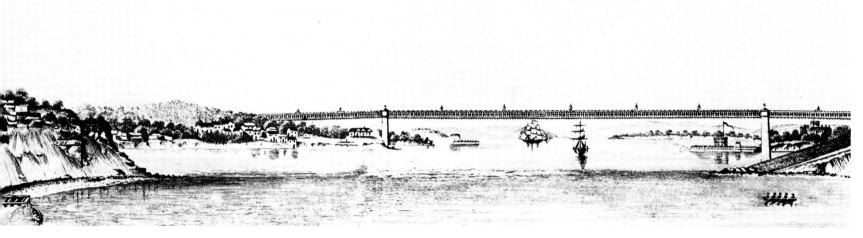

Plate 123   PETER HENDERSON. **Harbour Bridge Proposal.** *Drawing. Mitchell Library.*

The first known drawing of a bridge to connect the city with the North Shore was made in 1857 by Peter Henderson of Minton Villa, Woolloomoolloo Bay. He had served his engineering apprenticeship in England under George Stephenson and worked with the flamboyant Isambard Kingdom Brunel, builder of so many English railway bridges and viaducts. His drawing is a wonderful baroque cast-iron fantasy complete with oil-lit coach lamps on the main pillars. Its enormous unsupported span of 1,650 feet would have made it a candidate for the world's most spectacular harbour bridge collapse, had Henderson ever been commissioned to build it. At this time there was very little geological information available regarding the rock structure below the ooze of the harbour bed, so Henderson probably believed it would have been impossible to build additional supporting pylons under his elegant bridge.

The first real proposal for a harbour bridge was made by Francis Greenway, Macquarie's Government Architect in 1815. Sadly his original drawings have been lost, but in a letter to *The Australian* in 1825 Greenway wrote "in the event of the Bridge being thrown across from Dawes Battery to the North Shore, a Town would be built (there) . . . that would give an idea of magnificence and reflect credit and glory on the Colony."

In January 1840, a naval architect named Robert Brindley proposed that Sydney should have a floating bridge 45 feet wide with a toll house on each shore. It was to be driven by steam and move at "incredible speed".

The idea of the bridge died down as the ferry services to the North Shore gradually improved but by 1879 T. S. Parrott had prepared an altogether more prosaic drawing for a truss bridge of 7 spans from Dawes Point, the longest span being 500 feet. However his drawing lacks the charming details of Henderson's with its boats full of naval officers, resplendent in cocked hats rowing past Miller's Point. T. S. Parrott's design was hotly debated and then quietly shelved. It was to be 32 years before J. J. C. Bradfield made his first proposals, which led to the building of the Harbour Bridge which changed the face of The Rocks forever.

Genesis and Growth 1788-1888

Plate 124   CAPTAIN JOHN HUNTER **Sydney Cove, August 20, 1788.** *Engraving. Author's collection.*

JOSEPH LYCETT. **Sydney Cove from Kirribilli. 1824.** *Aquatint. Mitchell Library*

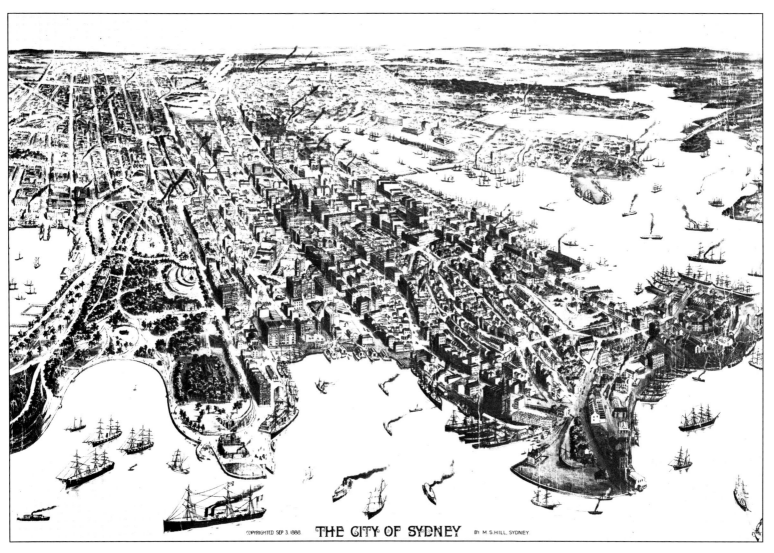

COPYRIGHTED SEP 3. 1888.   THE CITY OF SYDNEY   BY M.S.HILL, SYDNEY.

Plate 125   *M. S. HILL.* **The City of Sydney.** *Lithograph. Mitchell Library.* □ *In August 1788 Captain John Hunter drew the freshwater Tank Stream and the fine harbour, which were responsible for Governor Phillip's decision to move to Sydney Cove from Botany Bay. Joseph Lycett showed the development that took place during the next thirty years.*

The bird's eye panorama shows how dramatically the city changed by the end of its first century. The Tank Stream disappeared underground and its estuary became the Circular Quay with its wharves and ferry terminals. Pyrmont Bridge appeared in Hill's panorama, linking busy Darling Harbour to Glebe and Balmain, and the railway opened up development in the Western Suburbs. Smoking chimneys all around the lithographed view show that Sydney had now become a thriving commercial city, rather than the port and market town drawn by Lycett. The population of the suburbs doubled in the 1880s and terrace housing replaced the old colonial cottages with their picket fences and shingled roofs. James Inglis could have been describing Hill's panorama when he proudly wrote "The overflow of bricks and mortar has spread like a lava-flood . . . till the houses now . . . succeed each other row after row, street after street. Brickyards are worked to their utmost capacity; iron foundries are taxed to their greatest powers, saw-mills and joinery establishments are in full activity and the building trades are in constant employment."

155

Bibliography

In compiling this historical outline of Sydney from early paintings, the author has consulted both unpublished and published materials. Naturally the standard journals of the First Fleet such as *Watkin Tench, Phillip, John White, John Hunter and David Collins* have been used as basic reference sources, as has the Australian Dictionary of National Biography. Some of the unpublished and secondary source materials are also listed here, but it would be impossible to include all reference sources used.

Unpublished Manuscripts ML = Mitchell Library DL = Dixson Library

Angas, George French. Papers. ML MS Aa/11
Bligh Papers. Documentation on Arrest of Governor Bligh by George Johnson ML D357
Dixson, Sir William. "Notes and key to Evans' View of Sydney Cove." DL MSQ 35F
Elyard, Samuel. "Diary and Family Papers." Dixson Library MSS 592/115-122 MS Q217-235
Hardwick, John W. "Letters" ML MSS 448
Huey, Lieutenant Alexander. Diary. Public Record Office of Northern Ireland, Belfast.
Jevons, William S. "Social Survey of Sydney" ML B/864
MacLeay, Alexander. Vols. of correspondence with MacArthur papers ML A4300-4313
Martens, Conrad "Notebooks & Letterbooks" DL MS 142-4
Martens, Conrad "Account of Pictures painted in Sydney," DL MS 142
Stobart, Henry "Journal of a Visit to New South Wales, November 1852-1857." July 1853. ML MSS 1229.
Stobart Henry "Letters and Journal" ML Microfilm FM 2129.

JOURNALS AND NEWSPAPERS

Art and Australia. March 1983. Watkins, J. "Samuel Elyard."
Journal of the Australian Historical Society (later Royal Australian Historical Society). Sydney 1901-1980
Australian, Sydney. 1824-48. *Illustrated Sydney News.* Sydney. 1853-1894.
Sydney Gazette and New South Wales Advertiser, Sydney. 1803-1842. *Sydney Echo,* April 25, 1890. *Sydney Herald & Sydney Morning Herald.*

BOOKS

Arago, Jacques. *Promenade autour du monde.* Paris 1822.
Chapman, Don. *The People of the First Fleet.* Sydney. Cassell, 1981.
Dumont D'Urville, J. S. C. *Voyage pittoresque autour du monde* Paris 1834-5.
Benezit, Emmanuel. *Dictionnaire critique et documentaire des peintres... Paris,* Grund. 1976.
Bertie, C. H. *The Story of Old George Street.* Sydney. Tyrells. n. d.
Cunningham, Peter. *Two years in New South Wales.* London 1827.
Dutton, Geoffrey. *The paintings of S. T. Gill.* Adelaide 1957.
Fairfax, J. F. *The Story of John Fairfax.* Sydney. J. Fairfax. 1941.
Fisher, G. L. *The University of Sydney. 1850-1875.* Sydney. University Press, 1975.

Flower, Cedric. *The Antipodes Observed.* Melbourne, Macmillan, 1975.
Fowles, Joseph. *Sydney in 1848.* Sydney, 1848.
Fox, Len. *Old Sydney Windmills.* Sydney, Len Fox 1978.
Gibbs, Shallard. *Illustrated Guide to Sydney.* Sydney, 1882.
Gillespie, Rollo. *Vice-Regal Quarters.* Sydney, Angus & Robertson, 1975.
Hackforth-Jones, Jocelyn. *Augustus Earle, Travel Artist.* Canberra, Angus & Robertson, 1980.
Hackforth-Jones, Jocelyn. *The Convict Artists.* MacMillan Co. Melbourne, 1977.
Hermann, Morton. *Early Australian Architects & their Work.* Sydney, Angus & Robertson, 1954.
Max Kelly. *Paddock Full of Houses.* Sydney, Doak Press, 1978.
Kerr, Joan & Broadbent, James. *Gothic Taste in the Colony of New South Wales.* Sydney, David Ell. 1980.
Lindsay, Lionel. *Conrad Martens. The Man and his Art.* Sydney. Angus and Robertson. 1968.
Lubbock, Adelaide. *Owen Stanley, R. N.* Melbourne, Heinemann, 1968.
Lycett, Joseph. *Views in Australia or N.S. Wales delineated in 50 views.* London 1824.
Maclehose, James. *Picture of Sydney & Strangers' Guide in New South Wales for 1839.* Sydney 1839.
Malaspina, Alejandro. *Viaje politico-cientifico alrededor del mundo. 1788-94.* Madrid 1853.
McCulloch, Alan. *Encyclopaedia of Australian Art.* Melbourne, Hutchinson, 1968.
McCulloch, Alan. *Artists of the Australian Gold Rush.* Melbourne, Lansdowne, 1977.
McCulloch, Alan. *Encyclopaedia of Australian Art.* Sydney, Hutchinson, 1977.
Moore, William. *The Story of Australian Art.* Sydney. Angus & Robertson 1934.
Mourot, Suzanne. *This was Sydney.* Sydney. Ure Smith, 1969.
Mundy, G. C. *Our Antipodes.* London 1852.
Newman, C. E. T. *The Spirit of Wharf House.* Sydney, Angus & Robertson, 1961.
Park, Ruth. *Companion Guide to Sydney.* Sydney. Collins, 1983.
Peron, Francois & Freycinet, Louis. *Voyage des decouvertes or Voyage of discovery to the Southern Hemisphere by order of the Emperor Napoleon.* London, 1809.
Rienits, Rex & Thea. *Early Artists of Australia.* Sydney, Angus & Robertson, 1963.
Stephensen, P. R. *History and Description of Sydney Harbour.* Adelaide, Rigby. 1966.
Thieme, Ulrich und Becker, Felix. *Allgemeines Lexicon der bildenden Kunstler* Leipzig, Seemann. 1967-71.
Watling, Thomas. *Letters from an Exile at Botany Bay to his Aunt in Dumfries.* Perth. c.1794.
Watson, Frederick. *The History of the Sydney Hospital.* Sydney, 1911.

Acknowledgements

In order to fit the format of the book it has sometimes not been possible to include the complete work but where a minor portion only has been included, this has been noted as a detail from the particular work.

The Mitchell Library and the Dixson Galleries are the major sources for the illustrations in this book and without the kind co-operation of the Trustees, this book could not have been compiled. The author is most grateful for the help provided by Margaret Calder, Paulette Jones and Shirley Humphries and the staff of the Mitchell Reference desk. Thanks are also due to Mary Vinten of the Stanton Library, North Sydney, Barbara Perry, Jean Trotman and Sylvia Carr of the National Library of Australia, the Assistant Curator of Elizabeth Bay House, the City of Sydney Public Library for information concerning the Town Hall, Tony Vann Cremer, Historical Officer of Australia Post, the Curator of the Mint Museum, the Archives of the Customs Department and the Private Secretary to His Excellency the Governor of New South Wales for much valuable information concerning the building of Government House and its Bridge Street predecessor.

Mr Phillip Jago of the National Gallery of Victoria and the Directors of the Julian Ashton Art School kindly gave permission to reproduce the work by Julian Ashton and the Martens of Elizabeth Bay House. Kenneth Hince of Melbourne and Timothy McCormick of Paddington were also most helpful in allowing photographs of items of their stock to be taken.

To Joe Lebovic of the Josef Lebovic Gallery of Paddington, I express my sincerest thanks for his enthusiasm and assistance with the entire project from its inception and to Dinah Dysart of the National Trust for organising an exhibition based on the pictures in the book at the S. H. Ervin Museum and Art Gallery of the National Trust.

Additional thanks are also due to Lord Montagu of Beaulieu for the right to reproduce a portrait of Lord Henry Scott and for much valuable information about his grandfather, to Max Kelly of the History Department of Macquarie University for finding the Balcombe drawing and to Michael Reymond, who generously allowed access to his important research on Cleveland House and to architect, Howard Tanner for some helpful suggestions with the material.

Bryan and Zillah Thomas of Early Australia Maps and Charts kindly allowed their reconstructed map of the streets of Macquarie's Sydney to be published and thanks are also due to John Hawkins of Cammeray for his help with the publication of the Conrad Martens from the Australian Consolidated Press collection. Thanks, too, to Jonathan Watkins, formerly of the Power Institute of Fine Arts, for his invaluable assistance with research and for the inclusion of some of his own biography of Samuel Elyard from the most interesting exhibition of that artist's work which he organised. Colin Sheehan, John Oxley Librarian provided advice with the indexing, Commander Geoffrey Ingleton kindly allowed the inclusion of his etching of the Carters' Barracks Treadmill. Tony Wheeler of Pascoes was unfailingly helpful in organising for photography of many items and thanks are also due to Tony Carpenter for his photography of items at the Josef Lebovic Gallery. I should like to thank Michael Reymond for letting me use some of his valuable research into the history of Cleveland House and to regret that his name was inadvertently omitted from the first edition. Lastly, thanks go to my sister, Eileen, for her diligent research into the diary of Lieutenant Huey, as well as to the two psychiatrist friends who gave me their diagnostic opinions about Samuel Elyard.

Index

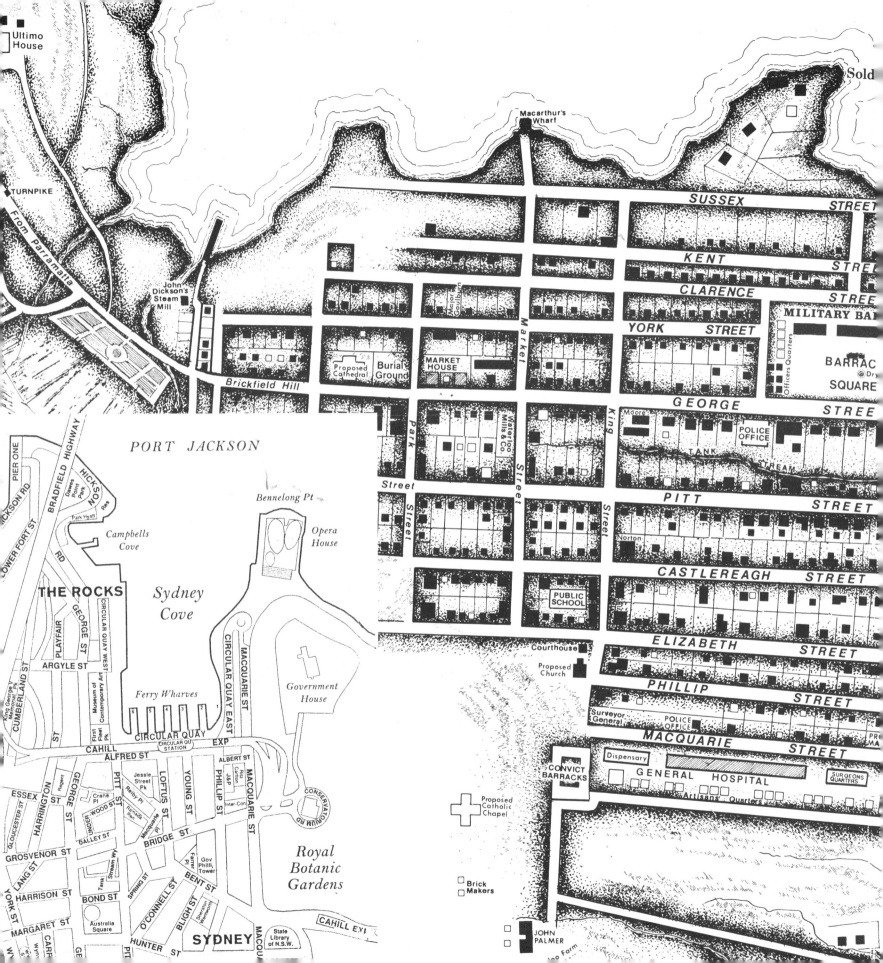